Frightfully Fun

Halloween

Crafts & Cooking

pil

Publications International, Ltd.

P9-CDW-263

Craft Designers: Paula Bales, 250, 254, 258, 260, 263, 268, 271; Amy Belonio, 8, 16, 20, 22, 61; Barb Chauncey, 264, 266, 267; Laurie D'Ambrosio, CHA, 18; Walter B. Fedyshyn, AIFD, PFCI, 64; Tom Fremgen, 272, 274, 276, 278; Steve Frey, 272, 274, 278, 280, 282; Lisa Galvin, 44, 47, 50, 68, 74; Gene Granata, 276, 278; Cindy Groom Harry® and Staff, Designs & Consultation, 77, 80, 83, 90; Diane Hardy, 248, 252, 253, 270; Megan Lacey, 71; Debi Linker, 66; Sharon Miller Cindrich, 14, 37, 42, 58; Sherri Osborn, 11, 86; Arlana Patten, 25, 32; Kristi Richardson, 5, 38; Vicki Jackson Schweitzer, 28; Ed Smith, AIFD, 34; Kim Solga, 88; Suzonne Stirling, 53, 56, 247, 248, 256, 262; Marge Wirsbinski, 40

Food Stylist: Kim Hartman/Modern Amalgamated Duo, Inc.

Models: Devin Anderson/Royal Model Management; Ramie Bagin/Lori Lins Ltd.; Theresa Lesniak; David McCoy/ Stewart Talent; Joel Sanchez/Stewart Talent; Kate Speare/ Lori Lins Ltd.; Megan Wharrie/Stewart Talent; Mark Wilson/ Stewart Talent

Photography: Andrews Braddy Photography; Art Explosion; Artville; Brand X Pictures; Glow Images; iStockphoto; Photos To Go; PDR Productions, Inc.; Richard Tragresser and Cindy Trim/Sacco Productions, Limited, Chicago; Shutterstock; Siede Preis Photography; Silver Lining Digital, Inc.; Brian Warling/Warling Studios

Prop Stylists: Melissa J. Frisco, Sally Grimes, Donna Preis, Lisa Wright/Redbird Visual Communications, Missy Sacco, Sheila Scatchell/Sheila Styling, Paula Walters

Technical Editor: Janelle Hayes

Front cover (*clockwise from top left*): Frankenstein Brains, 32; Halloween Spooktacular, 64; Slinky Snake, 40; Spooky Tic-Tac-Toe, 90

Back cover (*clockwise from top left*): Henrietta Witch, 28; Slimy Sliders, 170; Funny Faces, 274; Candy Corn Cookies, 222

Microwave Cooking: Microwave ovens vary in wattag Use the cooking times as guidelines and check for doneness before adding more time.

Preparation/Cooking Times: Preparation times are based on the approximate amount of time required to assemble the recipe before cooking, baking, chilling, or serving. These times include preparation steps such as measuring, chopping, and mixing. The fact that some preparations and cooking can be done simultaneously is taken into account. Preparation of optional ingredients a serving suggestions is not included.

Louis Weber, CEO
Publications International, Ltd.
7373 North Cicero Avenue
Lincolnwood, Illinois 60712

Permission is never granted for commercial purposes.

ISBN-13: 978-1-4508-2277-0
ISBN-10: 1-4508-2277-0

Manufactured in China.

8 7 6 5 4 3 2 1

Library of Congress Control Number: 2011924928

Contents

Frightfully Festive Fun

A chill has crept into the dark night air, the harvest moon hangs low in the night sky, and the trees have cast off their leaves, baring crooked branches to creak and scrape at your windows and sound the season's call: Celebrate Halloween this year in a way that'll bring down the haunted house!

No more dishing out dull snacks or scurrying to decorate your home for the spookiest night of the year. Think of this book as your own personal idea factory. We've drummed up the sweet, the scary, and the most spooktacular hit-makers to help you celebrate Halloween in high style. All you have to do is pick one idea—or a bunch of ideas—and put it into action. Creepy crafts, frightfully fabulous foods, creepily creative costumes, and phantastical pumpkins—they're all here.

The dreadfully delicious recipe sections are full of tasty treats. Your guests will be "goblin" them up before you can say "bone" appétit! From Finger Foods, serve Crispy Goblin Chips and Dinosaur Eggs for a fun brunch. Or how about Smashed Thumbsticks with Oily Dripping Sauce or Bloody Monster Claws to satisfy the ghoul in us all? (When we said *Finger* Foods, we really meant it!)

In Kooky Entrées, you'll find Chiles of Doom and Slimy Sliders. The Mini Pickle Sea Monster Burgers are bound to be a big hit with the kids. Yummy!

Your sinister sweet tooth will be satisfied with the delectable desserts in Sips 'n' Sweets. Try th Popcorn Ghosts or Spider Cakes for some swee morsels of deliciousness. Thirsty? What ghoul isn't? Try the Bloody Blast or Bobbing Head Punch to quench your parched throat.

Once you've had some spooky sustenance, you be ready to delve into the Halloween crafts. Make a freakishly fashionable statement with ou simple directions for knitting up an orange or black monster scarf. A Spooky House Centerpie can decorate your table. Slinky Snakes, BOO! Pots, and many more crafts await you.

Do your kids want to be werewolves, skeletons or maybe Little Bo Peep this Halloween? We've got easy instructions for scary or not-so-scary costumes. And no Halloween is complete without some jolly or jeering jack-o'-lanterns. Lots of pumpkin patterns are provided.

Make no mistake about it, ghouls and ghosts, there's fun to be had with *Frightfully Fun Halloween Crafts & Cooking.* With it, you can scare up some wicked Halloween mischief!

4

Horrifyingly Cool Crafts

"Handy" Halloween Centerpiece

This centerpiece is hands-on fun for the entire ghostly crew!

What You'll Need

- Black acrylic paint
- Paintbrush
- 6-inch papier-mâché box
- 6×3-inch wood rectangle
- Flat wood craft stick
- Hot glue gun, glue sticks
- Anchor pin
- Serrated knife
- Foam block
- Spanish moss
- 10 fern pins
- Fake hand
- Dowel rod, ¼ diameter, cut to 8 inches long
- Heavy-duty scissors
- Orange branches
- Rose stem
- Wired curly willow branches
- Brown astilbe stem
- Scrapbooking Halloween cutout

1 Paint box, wood rectangle, and flat stick black. Let dry. Apply second coat if needed for complete coverage.

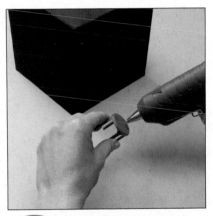

2 Glue anchor pin to inside bottom of box. Cut foam block to fit inside box; place foam on anchor pin. Cover foam with Spanish moss and secure with fern pins.

3 Cut a piece of foam to fit inside opening of hand; be sure foam fits snugly to hold hand's shape. Place foam inside hand opening.

4 Push dowel rod into foam inside hand, pushing dowel to top of hand.

5

5 Cut orange branches to varying lengths. Glue branches directly into foam throughout arrangement. Cut rose stem to varying lengths, and glue throughout.

6 Cut curly willow branches to varying lengths. Glue willow throughout arrangement. Pull astilbe from stem. Glue astilbe throughout. Insert and glue hand into foam.

7 To make sign, glue flat stick to wood rectangle, making rectangle wider than it is long when attached to stick. Glue Halloween cutout to wood stick. Glue sign into foam.

It's Halloween!

Boo!

Ghoulish Glow Candles

Frighteningly fun candles are a great way to add moody lighting to your Halloween scene.

What You'll Need

- Scissors
- 4 pieces cardstock
- 4 assorted pillar candles
- Ball-head stylus
- Paintbrush
- Black acrylic paint
- Craft eyelets
- Star brads
- Straight pins
- Colorful ball-head quilting pins
- Wire cutters
- Seed beads

1 Copy letter patterns on page 10 onto cardstock. Cut out inside of letters to create a stencil. Place each stencil on a candle, and mark outline with stylus. Use stylus to cut out letter about ⅛-inch deep. You may need to do a few passes over letters to get a good groove. Remove stencil. Don't worry if it looks less than spooktacular at this point—paint will cover faults. Use dry paintbrush to brush out shavings from grooves.

2 Paint in letter grooves with black acrylic paint; let dry. Repeat if necessary.

3 Push eyelets and star brads randomly into candles. Shorten straight and quilting pins with wire cutters so they are about ½ inch long. Randomly push quilting pins into candles. Place seed beads on straight pins, and push them into candles.

Note: Never leave a lit candle unattended.

Patterns are 100%.

Wacky Halloween Ornaments

Glass ball ornaments aren't just for Christmas anymore!
Use them to create a variety of fun decorations for Halloween.

What You'll Need

- 3-inch glass ball ornaments
- Acrylic paint: black, white, green, tan
- Paintbrush
- Craft foam, assorted colors
- Scissors
- Hot glue gun, glue sticks
- Fabric paint: black, yellow
- Accessories: yarn, craft wire, feather

1 Remove top and hanger from ornaments. Drizzle paint inside each ornament (see specific ornament directions for color instructions). Roll ornaments around to completely coat insides; add more paint if needed. Let ornaments stand for 3 or 4 days, until paint is completely dry.

2 Paint eyes, mouth, teeth, and other features on outside of ornament. Place ornament on cup to dry.

3 Cut out shapes from craft foam. Glue these and other items on ornaments to add features. Examples are given, but create your own monster or ghoul!

Bat: Paint inside black. Paint face. Cut 2 wings from black craft foam. Add accents to the wings using black fabric paint. Hot glue wings in place.

Witch: Paint inside green. Cut nose from green craft foam, gently fold down center, and glue in place. Use black fabric paint to make mole on nose. Paint face. Cut witch's hat and brim from black craft foam, and glue together. Cut 6-inch pieces of black yarn for hair, and glue in place. Glue hat to witch's head.

Wizard: Paint inside tan. Paint face. Cut wizard's hat from blue craft foam, and paint stars using yellow fabric paint. Glue hat together. Cut 6-inch pieces of white or gray yarn, and glue in place for hair. Glue hat on head. Shape glasses from a 6-inch piece of silver wire; glue glasses to head.

Pirate: Paint inside tan. Pain face (only paint 1 eye), addin dots of stubble. Cut three 4×1½-inch rectangles from brown craft foam for pirate's hat. Scallop top edge of rectangles. Glue ends togethe to form hat, and glue feather to hat. Glue hat to pirate's head. Cut out black eye patch and glue on.

Glass Bead Spider

Glittering spiders decorate your house and surprise your family with their realism.

What You'll Need

- Black round bead
- Teardrop glass bead with black and silver inside
- 26-gauge black wire
- Black seed beads
- Scissors or wire cutters

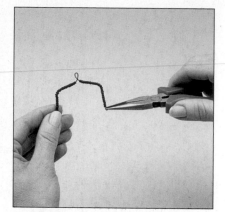

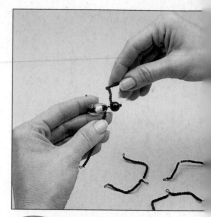

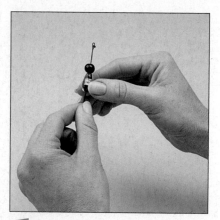

1 To make spider body, thread 6 inches of wire through large black bead and teardrop bead. Add a seed bead to end, thread wire back through both beads, and add another seed bead. Beads should not be tight against each other. Twist wires at end of spider, and insert wire ends into spider body.

2 Legs are made in pairs. Cut 6 inches of wire, and turn up an end. String on 25 beads. Fold wire in half, and leave about ¼-inch space unstrung. String 25 beads on other half of wire. Bend wire at end and trim. Make 2 pairs of legs. Make 2 more pairs of legs, threading 30 beads on each side.

3 Twist beaded legs (with longer legs toward back) around spider between large beads of body. Bend legs to make them spiderlike.

Haunted Tip

You can add a spider to your lapel—it's as simple as gluing a jewelry pin to the underside of a beaded spider!

Bewitching Branch

This glittery tree is so fun that you won't want to put it away when Halloween is over!

What You'll Need

- 6-inch terra-cotta pot
- Painter's tape
- Acrylic paint: black, orange, purple, silver
- Foam brush
- Firm tree branch
- Spray paint: black, glitter
- 5-inch foam ball
- Crinkle filler paper
- Purple eyelash yarn scrap
- Silver spiral tinsel
- Craft wire
- Wire cutters
- Needle-nose jewelry pliers
- Seed beads: assorted sizes in Halloween colors
- Assorted trinkets: beads, buttons, charms, small toys, Halloween confetti, etc.

1 Use painter's tape to create stripes around pot. Paint alternating black, orange, purple, and silver stripes. Let dry. Spray tree branch with black paint; let dry. Spray branch with glitter. Let dry.

2 Push foam ball into base of pot. Scatter crinkle paper on top to hide foam. Push branch into foam ball. Arrange crinkle paper if necessary.

3 Drape eyelash yarn in and around branches as a garland. Wrap silver spiral tinsel around branches and base.

4 Cut a 22-inch length of wire, and make a loop at an end. String beads onto craft wire in whatever pattern you'd like. When wire is almost covered, make a loop of wire at end. String beaded wire onto branch as a garland.

5 String trinkets onto pieces of wire to create ornaments. Twist a wire end into a loop around trinkets, then create a circle loop at other wire end. Cut excess wire. Decorate branch with trinkets.

Fuzzy Fun Wreath

Tired of the same ghosts and ghouls every year? Mix things up this Halloween by costuming your front door in this fantastically furry wreath!

What You'll Need

- Orange paper twist
- Scissors
- Straw wreath
- Hot glue gun, glue sticks
- Black spray paint
- Lime green fun fur yarn
- Pencil
- White foam core board
- Knife tool or craft knife
- Acrylic paint: gray, black
- Stencil brush
- Oval wiggle eyes: 4 small, 13 to 15 medium

1 Cut paper twist into approximately 1-yard-long pieces and untwist. Wrap paper twist around wreath, securing ends on back of wreath with glue.

2 Place wreath on newspaper in a well-ventilated area. Lightly spray-paint wreath—you just want small dots of black, not total coverage. Let paint dry. Wrap wreath with yarn; secure ends of yarn on back of wreath with glue. Double a 24-inch piece of yarn, and glue it to back of wreath for a hanger.

3 Using patterns, trace 1 large ghost and 2 small ghosts on foam core. Cut out. Lightly stipple gray

paint around edges of ghosts with stencil brush.

4 Set small wiggle eyes on small ghosts, and trace around eyes with pencil. Do the same with medium eyes and large ghost. Paint traced ovals black, painting slightly outside traced line. Paint mouth on large ghost. Let paint dry. Glue eyes on ghosts.

5 Glue ghosts to wreath with large ghost at top center and small ghosts to each side. Glue remaining wiggle eyes to wreath.

6 Make a bow from untwisted paper twist and yarn. Glue to bottom of wreath.

Enlarge patterns 300%.

Bewitching Hour

This terrifying time-teller will mesmerize your guests as the haunted hours pass!

What You'll Need

- 6½-inch unfinished wood circular clock
- Acrylic paint: white, orange, aqua, purple, lime green, black
- Paintbrushes
- Compass (optional)
- Pencil
- Light cardboard
- Craft knife
- ½-inch painter's tape
- Ribbons and yarn, assorted
- Scissors
- Heavy-duty stapler
- Halloween-themed charms, beads, brads, foam details

1 Basecoat clock with white; let dry.

2 Paint clock face orange. Let dry. Freehand or use compass, starting in center, to lightly draw 1⅛-inch, 2½-inch, and 5-inch circles. (Note: Place a small piece of cardboard in center of clock if using a compass.) Paint inner circle aqua. Let paint dry before painting next circle purple, and next circle lime green. Leave last circle orange.

3 Using word patterns on page 24, trace words on light cardboard. Cut out inside of letters using craft knife to make a stencil. Place "bewitching" on outer orange ring, and stencil with black. Place "hour" directly below "bewitching" in bottom part of orange circle, and stencil it black. Let dry.

4 Dip end of large paintbrush into aqua paint, and dot at 12, 3, 6, and 9 o'clock, redipping brush end after each dot. Repeat with a smaller brush, using lime green, and make dots at 1, 5, 7, and 11 o'clock. Using smallest brush and purple, make dots at 2, 4, 8, and 10 o'clock.

5 Tape outer edge of clock starting at top center, placing tape about every 1½ inches, making 8 sections. Between tape, paint orange, lime, aqua, and purple; let dry. Apply another coat of paint; let dry. Remove tape, allowing white stripes to show through.

6 Cut varying lengths of yarn and wire-edged and curling ribbon. Staple ends of all ribbon/yarn pieces to bottom back of clock. Use scissors to curl ribbons that can be curled, and twist and curl wire-edged ribbons. Attach various charms and embellishments along lengths of ribbons and yarns.

7 Cut a 24-inch length of ribbon. Tie middle of ribbon into bow, and double-knot it. Staple loose ends to top back of clock for a hanger. Attach clock works to clock as instructed in manufacturer's directions.

bewitching hour

Patterns are 100%.

Tomb Many Days to Count

Count down the days to Halloween on this funny mummy's tummy!

What You'll Need

- Craft chipboard (or cereal box)
- Craft glue
- Scissors
- 5×7-inch chalkboard
- Batting or stuffing scraps
- 1 yard muslin
- Stamp pads: antique linen, vintage photo, black soot
- Alphabet rubber stamps
- 2⅜×4-inch scrapbook tag
- Hemp cord
- 2 wiggle eyes, 25mm each
- 3 black brads
- Black fine-point marker
- 20-gauge black wire
- Chalk

1 Glue chipboard together, doubling the thickness. Using patterns on page 26, trace and cut out shapes from chipboard.

2 Glue head to top of chalkboard, arms to sides, and legs to bottom. Glue batting to chipboard pieces. Let dry.

3 Tear 2-inch-wide strips from muslin. Tie strip ends together to make 1 long strip. Wrap muslin around mummy, covering all chipboard pieces. Glue strips of fabric over wood of chalkboard to cover.

4 Distress mummy with antique linen ink. Distress tag with antique linen and vintage photo ink. Stamp words on tag using black soot ink. Tie 2 pieces of hemp cord to tag, and attach tag to mummy's arm. Tie knots in hemp.

5 Glue eyes onto head. Attach a brad at shoulder and another on leg. Attach last brad to top of tag. Use marker to draw spider legs beside brads. Tie wire around neck, and wrap wire around chalk.

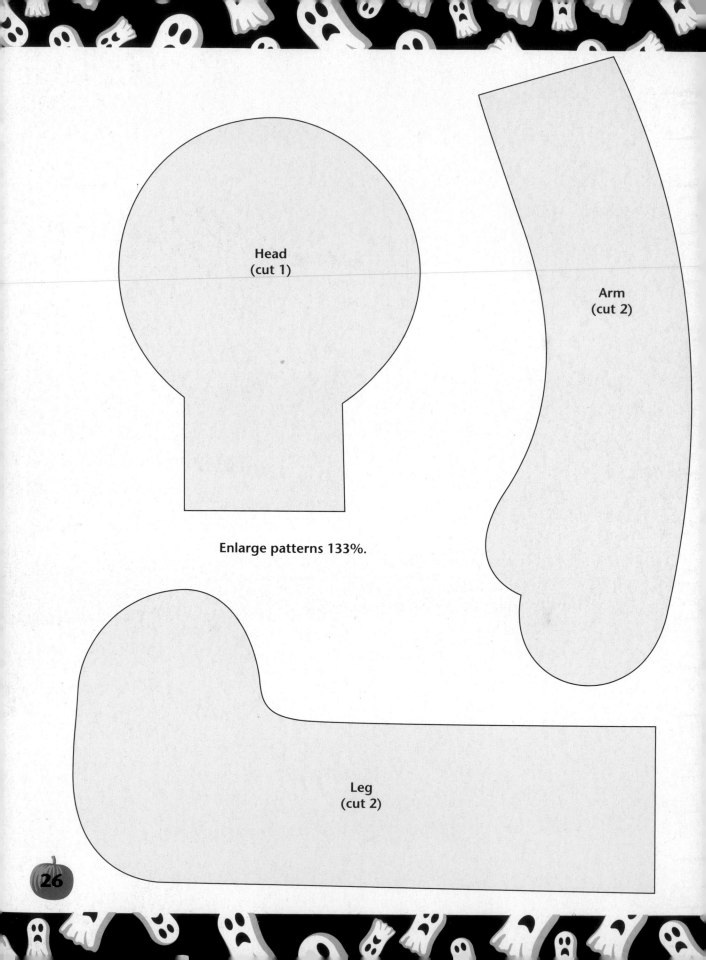

Head
(cut 1)

Arm
(cut 2)

Enlarge patterns 133%.

Leg
(cut 2)

26

Henrietta Witch

Henrietta is a nice witch, even though she is ready to fly away to her Halloween haunts at any minute! She is sure to delight all your little ghosts and goblins.

What You'll Need

- ¼ yard unbleached muslin
- 1 package tan dye
- Plastic or cardboard
- Scissors
- Water-erasable marker, fabric marking pencil
- Sewing machine
- Cream thread
- 10 ounces polyester fiberfill
- Pins
- ¼ yard each fabric: black, brown and black check, brown plaid
- 2 black seed beads
- 10 inches red embroidery floss
- Blusher
- 1 ounce wool roving for hair
- White craft glue
- ½ yard black ribbon, ⅛ inch wide
- 9-inch wood meat skewer
- 1½×4-inch piece gold-brown fabric

1 Wash and dry muslin; do not use fabric softener. Following manufacturer's directions, dye muslin.

2 Trace and cut all pattern pieces on page 31 onto cardboard or plastic. Leg-shoe is one piece, and seam line is marked.

3 With muslin folded (9×22-inches), trace arms and head-body pieces, leaving ½ inch between pieces. Traced lines are seam lines. Cut around all pieces ¼ inch away from seam lines.

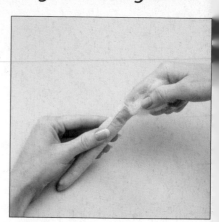

4 Stitch around arms, leaving top open. Clip curves, and turn right side out. Stuff to 1 inch below top. Baste top closed.

5 Stitch from A to B around head. Pin arms in place at sides. Stitch sides, catching arms in seams. Clip curves, and turn right side out.

Hem neck opening. Place dress on doll and gather at neck and sleeves above fringe.

12 Cut front vest at fold line. Hem vest armholes, neck, front, and bottom. Stitch shoulder seams. Place vest on doll.

6 Cut 2½×15-inch piece from black fabric, and cut 9×15-inch piece from muslin. Stitch pieces together along 15-inch side, and press seam toward black fabric. On wrong side of doubled fabric, trace leg-shoe twice, lining up seam line with seam. (Remember to leave ½ inch between pieces.) Cut out leg-shoe pieces ¼ inch from traced lines.

7 Stitch around leg-shoe on traced lines, leaving top open. Clip curves, and turn right side out. Stuff to 1½ inches below top. Place seams side by side and baste across the top.

8 Stitch legs to front body at opening, making sure feet are forward. Stuff head and body, and stitch opening closed.

9 Pinch face together to form nose; take 2 stitches through pinched fabric and fiberfill. Stitch on seed beads for eyes. With red floss, embroider mouth. Using finger, put blush on cheeks.

10 Trace and cut out dress and sleeves from check fabric, vest from plaid, and hat from black.

11 Stitch dress at shoulder seams, and stitch sleeves to dress. Fringe bottom of sleeves by cutting slits 1 inch deep and ¼ inch apart. Stitch sleeve and side seams. Fringe bottom of dress in the same manner as sleeves.

13 Using craft glue, glue wool roving on doll to form hair. Use fingers to lightly comb hair. Stitch back seam on hat, and turn right side out. Turn brim of hat up in front and glue in place. Glue hat on doll's head. Tie black ribbon into a bow and glue to front neck of dress.

14 Fringe gold-brown fabric in same manner as sleeves. Glue to end of meat skewer. Roll fabric around bottom of skewer, gluing as you roll to form broom. Stitch broom to hands at thumbs.

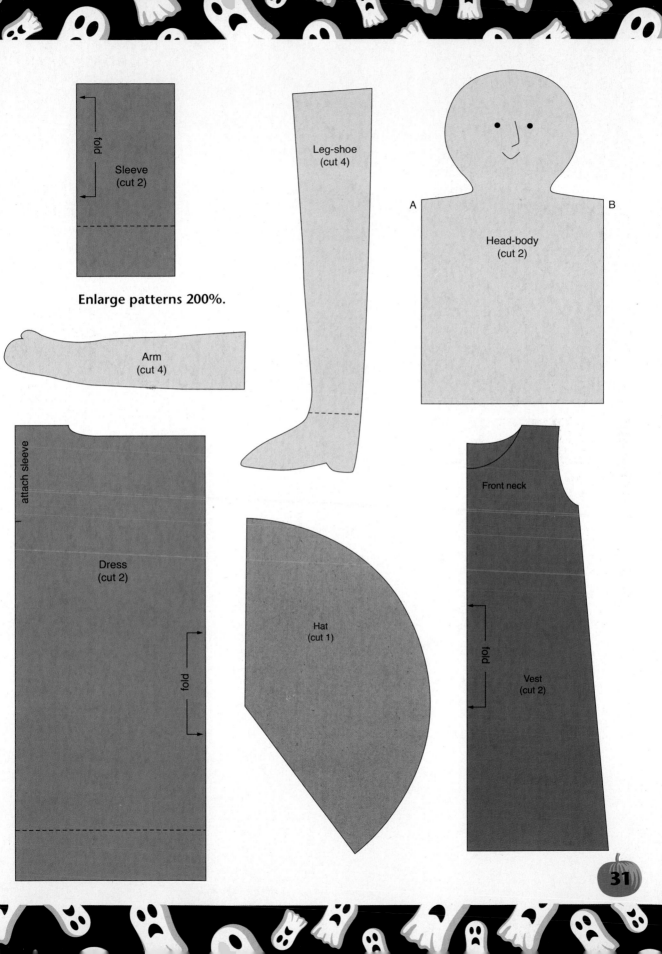

Sleeve
(cut 2)

fold

Enlarge patterns 200%.

Arm
(cut 4)

Leg-shoe
(cut 4)

A   B

Head-body
(cut 2)

attach sleeve

Dress
(cut 2)

fold

Hat
(cut 1)

Front neck

fold

Vest
(cut 2)

31

Frankenstein Brains

Frankly, it's a delight to serve a delicious concoction in Frankie's head.

What You'll Need

- 15-ounce clear plastic tumbler
- Blazing red solvent ink
- Watermark stamp pad
- Ultrathick embossing powder
- Heat gun
- Vegetable can
- Measuring tape
- Cardstock: 2 sheets green, scrap red, black
- Scissors
- Glue stick
- Red permanent marker
- Double-sided craft tape
- ½-inch hole punch
- 4 wiggle eyes
- Round-head machine screws with nuts

downward motion, use red solvent ink to make a dripping pattern. Let dry. Press stamp pad to ink, and sprinkle on embossing powder. Use heat gun to melt enamel.

2 Measure circumference and height of vegetable can. Divide circumference in half, and cut 2 pieces of green cardstock that size, adding 1×1¼-inch tabs on both sides of cardstock (about 2 inches down from top). Cut 2 tongues and 2 scars from red cardstock. Cut hair from black cardstock. Glue pieces to green cardstock pieces with glue stick. Add red lines through paper scars using marker. (You are making a front and back face.)

3 Add tape to back of green cardstock pieces do not place tape on ear tabs. Peel backing off tape, and place pieces on can, butting ear tabs. Punch a hole in middle of each ear tab.

4 Cover all paper with stamp pad and sprinkle on embossing powder. Use heat gun to melt embossing powder.

5 Glue on eyes. Add screws and nuts to holes in ears. Place tumbler on top of Frankenstein.

1 Working on outside of tumbler and using a

See Gucamole recipe on page 10

Boo Greetings

Let your guests know that all eyes are on them!
This decorative hanging will make everyone gasp (and gawk) at its beauty.

What You'll Need

- 5-inch wood letters: 1 B, 2 Os
- Orange spray paint
- 3 sheets black glitter felt, 9×12 inches
- Ruler
- Scissors
- Spray adhesive
- Foam, 12×18×1 inches
- 1 sheet neon-green felt, 9×12 inches
- Hot glue gun, glue sticks
- 2 frog wiggle eyes
- Silk autumn leaves
- 2 yards purple ribbon, 1½ inches wide
- 2 yards neon-green sheer ribbon, 1½ inches wide
- 2 chenille stems
- Large gerbera daisies: 1 orange, 2 purple
- Wire cutters
- 4 miniature orange gerbera daisies
- Small purple blossoms
- Assorted greenery
- Green berries
- Onion grass
- Floral U pins

1 In a well-ventilated area, following manufacturer's directions, spray wood letters orange. Let dry, and repeat.

2 Cut a sheet of black glitter felt into 1-inch strips. Spray strips and plain sides of 2 remaining felt sheets with adhesive. Spray edges and top of foam. Let spray adhesive become tacky. Place strips around edges of foam. Place 2 sheets of felt on top of foam, butting edges together. Trim felt if needed.

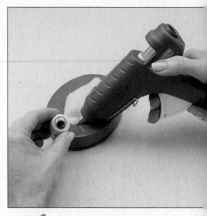

3 Cut 2 ovals of neon-green felt slightly larger than wood letter Os. Hot glue felt to inside of O, with felt puffing out front opening. Stuff O with felt scraps. Repeat for other O.

4 Insert and glue an eye in place at bottom of each O. Using photo as a guide, glue all letters to plaque.

5 Glue a cluster of autumn leaves on left edge of plaque and a small cluster to upper right corner. Cut a 12-inch length of both purple and green ribbon, and form each into a loop. Secure both with 2-inch length of chenille stem. Hot glue to upper right cluster.

6 Form remaining purple ribbon into a multiloop bow with 9-inch streamers. Secure bow with 2-inch length of chenille stem. Repeat for neon-green ribbon. Glue green bow on top of purple bow in middle of autumn leaves on left edge of plaque.

7 Cut stems of large gerbera daisies to about 3 inches. Insert and glue orange gerbera in center of bows; glue a purple gerbera below and slightly to the right of bow. Hint: Punch a tiny hole through felt to insert flowers into foam.

8 Using photo as a guide, insert miniature gerberas and larger purple gerbera in a line above bow. Fill in around flowers and bow with small purple flowers, assorted greenery, and green berries.

9 Curl grass by pulling across blade of scissors. Insert stems of onion grass as shown. V-cut ends of ribbons.

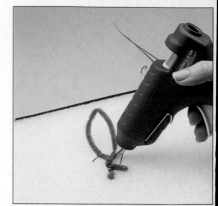

10 Form chenille stem into a loop, and insert in back of plaque as a hanger. Place U pins over hanger, and add glue to secure.

Monster Fur Scarf

A warm, furry monster hug—that's just what these scarves will feel like draped around your neck when there's a Halloween chill in the air!

What You'll Need

- Skein orange fun yarn (furry, eyelash, chenille, etc.)
- US size 11 knitting needles
- Scissors
- Monster claws
- Black embroidery floss
- Embroidery needle

1 Cast on 10 stitches. Knit all rows, using entire skein.

2 Sew 3 claws to each end of scarf.

Try This! Use a fun black yarn to knit the scarf. Glue on wiggle eyes for an eye-opening accessory.

Ghoulish Greeter

Sweep fall into your home with this uniquely scary door hanging.

What You'll Need

- Grapevine broom
- Plastic ghoul face
- 26-gauge green wire
- 2 orange berry branches
- Heavy-duty scissors
- Measuring tape
- Hot glue gun, glue sticks
- 5 purple ranunculus stems
- Fall leaf stem
- 46 inches double-faced black satin ribbon

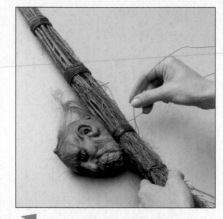

1 Wire face to broom. Cut berry branches into 4 sections of varying lengths, between 6 and 10 inches. Glue branches to grapevine.

2 Cut ranunculus stems to varying lengths, each between 3 and 8 inches. Glue ranunculus stems to grapevine.

3 Pull individual fall leaves off stem, and glue leaves throughout arrangement. Tuck leaf ends under flowers and berries.

4 Cut four 8-inch pieces of ribbon. From each piece, create a loop by gluing ends together. Glue ribbon loops behind face. Cut two 7-inch-long ribbons, and cut ends on an angle. Glue ribbons to arrangement below bow.

Slinky Snake

A slinky snake is a frightful sight, especially when coiled and ready to bite.
But have no fear, my dear, this slinky snake is made of rope, I hear!

What You'll Need

- Wire: 14 gauge, 24 gauge
- Yardstick
- Wire cutters
- Sandpaper
- 3 feet black braided rope, ⅝ inch diameter
- Paper clay
- Round toothpick
- Acrylic paint: black, yellow
- Paintbrushes: ¼-inch flat, #3

1 Cut a 3-foot, 3-inch piece of 14-gauge wire. Sand one end to a point. Push wire into rope, leaving 1½ inches of wire protruding on each end.

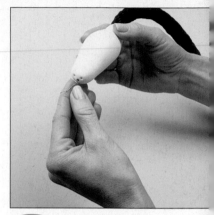

3 Cut two 1-inch pieces of 24-gauge wire. Twist wires together, leaving last ⅛ inch untwisted to form a forked tongue. Insert tongue into front of head. Use toothpick to make nostril holes. Let clay dry completely.

4 Use ¼-inch brush to paint head, tongue, and tail black. Use #3 brush to paint eyes yellow. Let dry.

5 Form body into a coil.

2 At each end, bend ½ inch of wire up. Mold head and tail onto wire with paper clay.

See Monster Munch recipe on page 126

Spooky Supperware

Add some cackles to your next Halloween meal—it'll be a real nail-biter! Guests will howl over this spooky set of ghoulishly fun utensils!

What You'll Need

- Green or white polymer clay (2-ounce pack per 2 utensils)
- Eating utensils
- Aluminum foil
- Baking pan
- Optional: Red or black nail polish

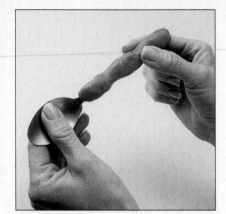

1 Preheat oven to 275°F. Condition clay until it is soft and pliable. Roll 1 ounce of clay into a log as long as utensil handle. Press handle front firmly into log, and work clay around back of handle until handle is covered. Shape clay to create bumpy knuckles.

2 Use a knife to make crease marks in knuckles. Press round edge of a spoon into fingertip end to make a fingernail.

3 Place finished utensils on aluminum foil on baking pan. Bake clay for 30 minutes.

4 Remove from oven, and let cool before using. Paint fingernails, if desired. Hand wash utensils.

Falling Leaf Garland

Hang this lovely garland from your mantle or use it in your next holiday table arrangement to bring the season to life.

What You'll Need

- 9¼×12-inch sheet lightweight copper sheeting (.003 thick, 40 gauge)
- Giant leaf paper punches
- Craft foam or stack of newspapers
- Blunt-tip stylus
- Embossing tool
- Metal baking sheet
- Disposable gloves
- Scrap paper
- Rub-on metallic finish
- Makeup sponge
- Paper towel
- 2 yards nontarnish brass wire, 18 gauge
- Wire cutters
- Round-nose jewelry pliers
- Assorted beads: brown, green, earth-tone colors
- Pencil or dowel
- Embroidery needle

1 Punch 12 to 15 leaves of assorted shapes from lightweight copper sheeting. Place leaves onto craft foam. Use blunt-tip stylus to emboss leaf veins in soft copper.

2 Place leaves on baking sheet and heat with embossing tool to burnish, varying color tones from bright copper to shades of orange, rust, bluish-purple, and gold. Repeat for all leaves. Let cool.

3 Place leaves on scrap paper. With gloved hands, use a makeup sponge to apply metallic finish. Let sit for 1 to 2 minutes, then wipe off excess with paper towel, buffing lightly while leaving color in grooves and corners. This gives a softened, antique look. Repeat for both sides of all leaves.

4 Use wire cutters to snip several 3- to 5-inch lengths from brass wire; set aside. To make garland, use round-nose pliers to curl a small loop at end of long brass wire. Slip a few beads onto opposite end of wire, and push them all the way down. Bend, curl, and loop wire as you go, adding beads wherever you want. Create spirals by wrapping wire around pencil or dowel.

5 Put leaves on craft foam sheet again. With embroidery needle, pierce a small hole near stem of each. Insert small piece of wire (from step 4) through each pierced hole; bend wire into "U" shape, and wrap it around itself to hold leaf in place. Slip a few beads onto remaining length. Attach this piece to garland, bending a small loop around garland wire to hold it in place. Repeat for all leaves, alternating shapes and spacing leaves along length of garland.

Boo! Pots

Looking for a quick-and-easy project that is sure to be an eye-catcher? Then here's Boo! to you with beads and pots.

What You'll Need

- 4×4×2-inch foam block
- Serrated knife
- 4 clay pots, 3 inches each
- Natural excelsior moss
- Ribbon: 36 inches green, ¾ inch wide; 36 inches purple wire-edged, 1½ inches wide
- Scissors
- Pencil
- 2 sheets double-sided super-sticky tape, 9×6 inches each
- Aluminum armature wire, ¹⁄₁₆ inch diameter
- Wire cutters
- Small hammer
- Glass or metal baking dish
- Assorted wiggle eyes, 3mm to 28mm
- Tiny glass marbles: purple, green
- Tiny green glass bead mix
- 18-gauge black wire
- Round-nose jewelry pliers
- Black E beads

1 Use serrated knife to cut foam block into 4 equal blocks. Insert a block into each clay pot, wedging it tightly inside. Remove foam, and trim so foam is ½ inch below top edge of pot. Replace foam in all pots.

2 Cover foam with excelsior moss. Tuck edges of moss around foam, covering foam completely.

3 Cut both ribbons in half. Wrap top edge of 2 pots with green ribbon, tie a knot, and V-cut ribbon ends. Repeat for remaining 2 pots using purple ribbon. Set pots aside.

4 Trace 4 Os, 2 Bs (flip pattern to make back of B), 2 exclamation points, and 2 dots onto super-sticky tape. (Patterns are on page 48.) Cut out.

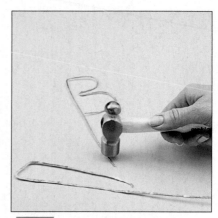

5 Shape aluminum wire into framework for letters and exclamation point, making framework ¼ inch smaller than shapes. Leave a 3½-inch tail at bottom of all shapes. Hammer wire flat.

7 Use front of shapes for this step. Remove protective layer from back of bead-coated shape, and place bead-side down onto a flat surface. Press framework onto sticky side. Replace protective layer. Attach framework to all letter fronts.

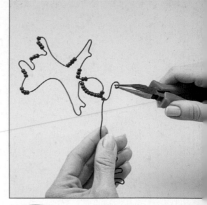

6 Place a B and a backward B in baking dish, and peel off top protective layer. Press wiggle eyes in place. Pour purple tiny glass marbles over tape to coat. Carefully press marbles onto front surface of B to fill any areas that weren't completely coated. Repeat process for all shapes. Note: For 2 Os (1 front and 1 back), use green glass bead mix, then fill in empty spaces with green glass marbles.

8 For backs of all letters, remove backing from unbeaded side. Take off protective layer from letter fronts, and apply matching back to each shape. Should edges not match exactly, press appropriate color beads or marbles to coat. Repeat for all shapes. Insert wire tails into clay pots.

9 Use jewelry pliers to bend and shape blac craft wire, creating spooky shapes. Thread E beads onto wire, and space them throughout shape. Cut wire end, and insert into clay pots.

Enlarge patterns 155%.

Candy Corn Jewelry

Get in the Halloween spirit with this sweet bracelet and earring set.
Make one set for yourself and another for a friend!

What You'll Need

- Freezer paper
- Masking tape
- Soft polymer clay: white, yellow, orange
- Acrylic clay roller
- Knife or cutting blade
- 18-gauge uncoated floral stem wire
- Baking pan (dedicated to polymer clay use)
- Polyester fiberfill
- 4 gold head pins, 2 inches long each
- Gloss varnish or lacquer
- Paintbrush
- 24 inches leather lace, 1mm round
- Round-nose jewelry pliers
- Lobster-style gold bracelet clasp
- Beads: frosted black pony, black E
- 8mm gold jump ring
- 2 (coiled) gold crimp-style cord ends
- Glue
- 2 gold wire earring hooks
- Wire cutters

1 Preheat oven to 265°F (or temperature indicated by clay manufacturer). Cover work surface with freezer paper, shiny side up. Tape in place.

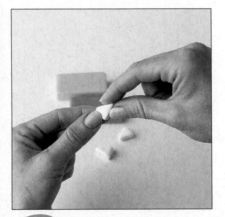

2 Knead 1-ounce block of white clay to condition, then roll on covered surface to create a pencil-size rope. Cut rope into ½-inch lengths. Pinch each ½-inch length between your fingers and thumbs to create 9 triangular candy corn pieces.

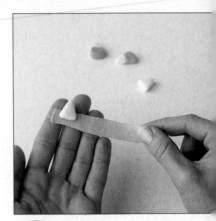

3 Condition yellow clay, then create a rope slightly smaller than a pencil in diameter. Roll rope flat using acrylic clay roller to create a thin strip of clay. With half of strip extending beyond wide end (base), wrap around each white triangle. Cut excess, and smooth with fingers.

6 Apply 2 to 3 coats of varnish. Let dry. Remove clay from wire and head pin.

4 Condition orange clay, and make a rope about the diameter of a pencil lead. Wrap around candy corn pieces between white and yellow. Press flat with fingers and smooth.

5 To create holes for jewelry, insert floral stem wire through sides of prepared candy corn pieces for bracelet; for earrings, beginning at narrow tip slip onto head pin. With pieces remaining on wire/pin lay onto fiberfill-lined baking tray, and bake as directed or for 25 to 30 minutes per ¼-inch clay thickness. Let cool.

7 Slip 1mm-round lace through coiled cord end then through loop at base of lobster claw. Pull lace through 3 to 4 inches, tie a knot, then return end through coil. Crimp coil end with pliers to hold round lace in place. Tie a knot at base of coil, then begin stringing beads as follows: E bead, pony bead, E bead, candy corn. Repeat to create desired bracelet length. Slip on remaining coil and jump ring. Pull lightly, and tie a knot attaching bracelet to jump ring. Slip remaining lace length back through coil and crimp end. Tie a knot at base of coil, add a drop of glue to secure, then cut excess lace at both ends of bracelet to finish.

8 For earrings, slip candy corn piece onto head pin. Add E bead, pony bead, then another E bead. Use jewelry pliers to bend loop at top. Cut excess with wire cutters, and slip loop onto earring hook and crimp to close, holding candy corn decoration in place on earring.

Festive Ware

Scare up an appetite with cookies served on easy-to-create painted glass plates.

What You'll Need

- Glass dinner plate
- Scissors
- Tape
- Enamel paint for tile, glass, or ceramic: dark green, yellow, orange, light green
- Fine-tip paint applicator
- Soft, natural fiber paintbrushes: 1 fine-tip, 1 flat

1 Photocopy pattern on page 54 several times so pattern will extend around plate. Cut out patterns, and tape around rim, with design facing down. Turn plate upside down.

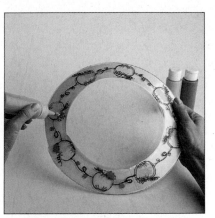

2 Begin painting by tracing vines with dark green paint and fine-tip applicator.

3 Using fine-tip brush and dark green paint, trace over veins in leaves. With fine-tip applicator and yellow paint, trace over accent lines on pumpkins. Using fine-tip applicator and orange paint, outline pumpkin shapes. Let paint dry 1 hour.

4 With fine-tip applicator and light green paint, trace over leaf outlines and fill in, covering the dark green veins on leaves. With flat brush, fill in pumpkin outlines with orange paint. Apply another coat after 15 to 20 minutes, if needed.

5 Finish by painting pumpkin stem with fine-tip brush and yellow paint. Air dry or bake (according to manufacturer's directions).

Attach an applicator tip to a bottle of black enamel paint. Paint over the horizontal and vertical lines. Add lines with paint, dividing each quarter until you have desired number of spokes (8 to 16). Now use paint to create webbing between the spokes. Work with 1 spoke at a time, turning plate as you go.

Let dry for 1 hour before adding spider. Spider is created with same applicator tip; draw an oval and fill in with paint. Add legs. Let dry or bake (according to manufacturer's directions).

Haunted Tips

- Occasionally wipe off applicator tip with damp paper towel to keep your lines clean.
- Use a toothpick to clean up any excess paint.
- If you are unhappy with your design, wash the plate before the paint dries (within 24 hours).

Note: Carefully hand-wash plates; do not use a dishwasher.

Try This!

Lure your guests into a web of goodies when they're displayed on this Spiderweb Plate. You'll need many of the same materials you used to create the Pumpkin Vine Plate, plus a disappearing ink pen. To decorate the plate, turn the plate bottom side up. Using the disappearing ink pen, draw a horizontal line across the center of the plate. Add a vertical line down the center.

Pattern is 100%.

See Autumn Leaves recipe on page 192

Fright Lights

Illuminate the night with simple silhouettes enhanced by vellum and candlelight.

What You'll Need

- White colored pencil
- Lightweight black paper
- Fine-tip scissors (such as embroidery scissors)
- Double-sided cellophane tape
- Ruler
- Rotary cutter or scissors
- 5 sheets orange vellum
- 3 heat-proof candleholders, 6 inches each
- 2 heat-proof candleholders, 8 inches each (use containers meant specifically for candles)
- Votive candles

1 Trace patterns onto black paper; cut out shapes with embroidery scissors. Use small pieces of double-sided tape to affix one shape to front of each candleholder.

2 Using ruler and rotary cutter or scissors, trim vellum so it just reaches top edge of candleholder but is no higher than lip of container.

3 Wrap vellum around candleholders, and secure at back with double-sided tape. Place candles in holders, and carefully light candles.

Enlarge patterns 145%.

Haunted Tip

As with any lit candles, do not leave them unattended, and do not use candles that rise over the rim of the containers.

Spooky House Centerpiece

A little Halloween magic transforms an ordinary wooden birdhouse into a charismatic cottage with a crooked chimney, spooky bat accents, and a glittery black roof.

What You'll Need

- Wooden birdhouse
- Needle-nose pliers
- Wood filler
- Sandpaper
- Acrylic paint: purple, black, yellow
- 4 foam paintbrushes
- Wooden star cutout
- Pencil or white colored pencil
- Lightweight cardboard or craft foam
- Construction paper: black, blue
- Scissors
- Craft glue
- Black modeling clay
- Hot glue gun, glue sticks
- Copper wire: 18 gauge, 22 gauge
- Ruler
- Wire cutters
- 7 silver star sequins
- Glitter: black, crystal
- Raffia: black, orange
- Floral accent pumpkin

1 If birdhouse has a perch, pull it out using needle-nose pliers. Fill hole with wood filler; let dry. Sand smooth.

2 Paint house purple and roof black. Paint wooden star yellow. Let dry.

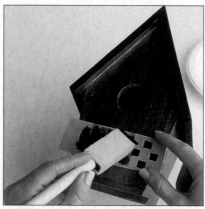

3 Draw a checkerboard pattern onto lightweight cardboard or craft foam; cut out. Stencil checks around middle of house using black paint. Let dry.

4 Trace door pattern on page 60 onto black construction paper; cut out. Use craft glue to glue door on front of house, covering hole and perch area.

5 Mold a crooked chimney out of modeling clay. Let harden for at least 8 hours. Hot-glue chimney to roof.

6 Cut 18-gauge wire into a 6-inch length, and bend into a curved line. Hot-glue this wire to back of wooden star. Stick other end deep inside chimney to hold in place.

7 Cut 22-gauge wire into 3 pieces, approximately 3 to 4 inches each. Bend into curvy lines. Sandwich one end of wire between 2 silver star sequins, and hot-glue 3 pieces together. Repeat with other 2 wires. Stick ends of wires deep into chimney.

8 Use a paintbrush to paint craft glue along sides and on top of roof. Generously sprinkle black glitter on glue. Put large glob of hot glue on top of chimney to secure wires, and sprinkle with black glitter.

9 Trace bat pattern onto blue construction paper 4 times; cut out. Fold them down middle, making creases. Dab wings with craft glue; sprinkle lightly with crystal glitter. Use hot glue to secure bats around house.

10 Hot-glue raffia around base of house. Hot-glue the floral pumpkin in place. Hot glue remaining star to door.

Patterns are 100%.

Creepy Coasters

These fun foam coasters do double duty as decor and surface-savers!

What You'll Need

- Craft foam: assorted colors (6mm and 2mm)
- Thin marker or pencil
- Fine scissors, craft knife
- Hole punches: 1/8 inch, 1/4 inch
- Foam glue
- Metallic gold acrylic paint
- Paintbrush

1 Cut all bases from 6mm foam. Using pattern base for wizard hat (see page 62), cut out a black base. Cut out a white 3¾-inch circle. Cut 2 black 3¾-inch squares.

2 Using patterns on page 62, cut out design shapes from 2mm craft foam with scissors and craft knife. Punch circles from 2mm craft foam in colors shown in photo.

3 Glue designs to corresponding foam bases. Paint some pirate's treasure gold. Let dry.

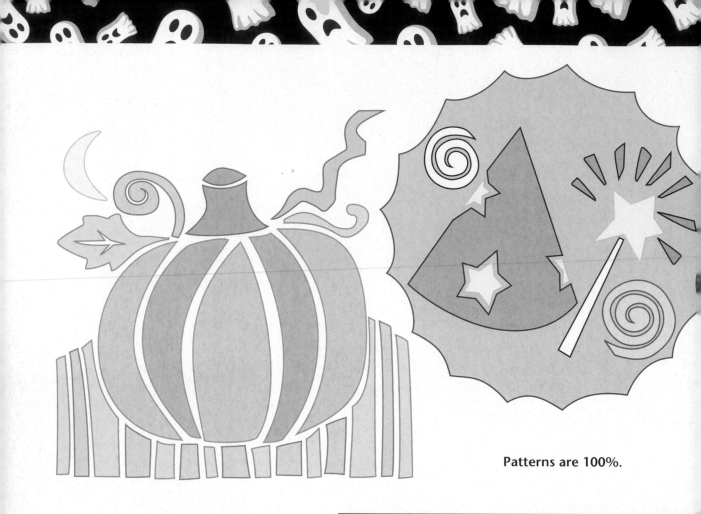

Patterns are 100%.

e Bloody Blast recipe on page 194.

Halloween Spooktacular

Spooky ghosts frolic with creepy black spiders and orange pumpkins on this wreath of crisp fall leaves. Hang it on your front door so these frightful fellows can tell trick-or-treaters, "Have a Happy Halloween!"

What You'll Need

- White tissue paper
- Ruler
- Scissors
- 6 white foam balls, 2 inches each
- Raffia
- Black fine-point felt-tip pen
- Hot glue gun, glue sticks
- Glass jar, with bottom at least 5 to 6 inches in diameter
- Water mister
- Paper towels
- 10 to 12 birch branches, 7 to 8 inches long
- Natural grapevine wreath, 18 inches
- Bunch dried fall leaves
- 3 medium artificial pumpkins
- 12 small artificial pumpkins
- 10 small black plastic spiders

1 Cut tissue paper into 15×15-inch square pieces; make 6 squares. Place a foam ball in center of paper, and gather paper over ball.

Smooth tissue over ball to form head of ghost. Tie tissue under ball with raffia. With pen, draw eyes, nose, and mouth.

2 With glue gun, "draw" a spiderweb shape on bottom of glass jar. The diameter of the web should be 4 to 5 inches. Spray with water, and let glue dry for 1 to 2 minutes. Carefully peel off web. Pat dry with paper towel. Make 4 to 6 webs. Color backs of webs with black pen.

3 Glue pieces of birch branches into grapevine wreath. Be sure to keep branches going in same direction around wreath.

4 Glue dried leaves ont wreath. Again, make sure they go around wreath i same direction.

5 Glue ghosts to wreath Make sure all ghosts are facing front. Glue in extra dried leaves as needed.

6 Glue pumpkins between ghosts. Ad extra leaves and branches as needed to hold pumpkins in place and to hide glue.

7 Slip spiderwebs over branches. Use small amount of hot glue to secure them to branches. Hot glue spiders around wreath.

64

Halloween Socks

Here's a project that'll knock your socks off! This embellished footwear can be the finishing touch for a costume or provide a subtle way to share your Halloween spirit. Treat your feet to something special.

What You'll Need

- 2 black socks
- Flat organza ribbon, 1⅜ inches wide (enough to go around the stretched edges of the sock ribbing)
- Sewing machine
- Needle and black thread
- Brass charms

1 Lay one sock at a time flat on work area. Do not fold cuff on sock. Stretch ribbing of sock, as shown.

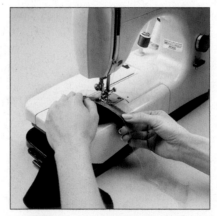

2 Position flat ribbon so approximately ¾ inch is over ribbing. Remainder of ribbon should extend off top of sock. This is how a double ruffle effect is achieved. With a sewing machine, straight stitch through ribbon along very outer edge of ribbing. Make sure to keep ribbing fully stretched while stitching. Ribbon will be ruffled when ribbing is returned to shape. Repeat steps 1 and 2 on second sock.

3 Turn down ribbing to form a cuff on both socks. Hand-stitch charms on turned-down cuffs so they show on ankles when worn.

Haunted Tip

When selecting the socks and
ribbon for this project, keep in
mind to choose materials that
wash well. You also may choose
to hand wash the finished socks
so the charms and ribbon are
subject to gentler conditions.

My Little Mummy

Not every aspect of Halloween has to be spooky. This little mummy would just love to hang around at your next holiday haunting!

What You'll Need

- Measuring cup
- 1-quart saucepan
- 5 tea bags
- ¾ yard unbleached muslin, 60 inches wide
- Scissors
- Iron, ironing board
- Straight pins
- Pencil with eraser end
- Sewing machine
- Coordinating thread
- Polyester fiberfill
- Sewing and embroidery needles
- 2 black E beads
- Spray bottle
- Paper towel
- Plastic clothes hanger
- 5×8-inch piece felt
- 6 old buttons, assorted sizes
- Yellow embroidery floss

1 Measure 3 cups of hot water into saucepan. Steep tea bags, and let cool while you create doll.

2 Use photocopier to enlarge doll body and tie pattern on page 70; cut out. Press muslin with iron if needed. Leaving a 2-inch border around all outside edges, pin body pattern to doubled layer of muslin. Use sharpened pencil to trace around pattern, directly onto muslin. Remove pattern. Pin arms, legs, head, and stomach to prevent layers from shifting during sewing. DO NOT cut out body yet.

3 Sew body, stitching directly on pencil lines and beginning and ending at dot between legs. Backstitch at beginning and end to prevent seam from unraveling. Cut out, leaving ¼-inch seam allowance around outside edge. Clip curves and inside corners to ease. Remove straight pins. Pinch only 1 layer of fabric at center of doll's back and cut a small slit (refer to pattern as a guide). Turn doll right side out through slit. Use eraser end of pencil to smooth head, arms, legs, and feet. Stuff with fiberfill. Eraser end of pencil can be used to push stuffing into extremities. Thread sewing needle with coordinating thread and whipstitch slit at back to clos

4 Stitch E beads to head for eyes. For a more dimensional effect, begin at back side of head: Inserting needle through to front side, slip on bead, then return needle through head to back side again. Pull to embed (or sculpt) eye into head. Repeat for remaining (bead) eye; whipstitch at back of head to secure thread ends.

5 Tear ten to twelve 1-inch-wide strips of muslin up to 60 inches long. Press if needed. Tie 3 knots in 1 strip to make hanger.

6 Begin wrapping mummy with all remaining strips, whipstitching a small dot at each end to hold firmly in place on doll. Once doll is partially wrapped, some ends can be tucked under other layers to hold in place or tied in some areas to create an "unraveling" appearance. Tie hanger to wrists as shown.

7 Remove tea bags from saucepan and discard. Pour tea into spray bottle, and with doll held over a sink or water basin, spray lightly with tea mixture. Coat outer layer only; do not completely saturate doll. Dab with paper towel to remove excess liquid, then reapply until desired effect is achieved. Hang doll from plastic clothes hanger until dry.

8 Pin tie pattern to felt and cut out. Cut a ½×8-inch strip of same felt fo neck portion of tie. Referring to dotted line on pattern, center top of necktie on felt strip. Fold top point of tie ove strip and stitch a button on top to hold in place. Tie thin strips of scrap felt to hanger t accent. Stitch buttons to doll with floss.

Enlarge patterns 155%.

Felted Autumn Pot Holders

These pot holders are quick and simple to make. Decorative details make them wonderful seasonal kitchen accessories.

What You'll Need

- Yarn: 100% wool worsted weight yarn, about 85 yards (78m) each in 3 colors

  We used: *Patons Classic Wool (100% wool; 223 yards [205m] per 3½ oz [100g] ball): #240 Leaf Green, #207 Rich Red, #204 Old Gold, 1 ball each*

- Needles: US size 7 (4.5mm)

- Notions: Tapestry needle; size 2 (2.5mm) steel crochet hook

Size: *Before felting: approximately 7½×8" (20×23cm); after felting (before crocheted border is applied): 6×6" (15×15cm)*

Gauge: *20 stitches and 26 rows=40 (10cm) in stockinette stitch*

Note: *Superwash wool and synthetics will not felt; do not use for felting projects.*

Pot Holders

Make the pot holders (make 1 in each color): Loosely cast on 40 stitches.

Row 1 (right side): Knit.

Row 2 (wrong side): Purl.

Repeat rows 1 and 2 for a total of 58 rows.

Bind off. Weave in all loose ends.

Felting

Note: The yarn type, washing machine, water temperature, and condition can all affect the felting process. Check the pieces at regular intervals to determine felting condition. If you need more than one full cycle, reset the machine and start again, checking frequently; if the project is felted to your satisfaction in less than a full cycle, rinse well without agitation, and remove it from the machine.

Using small load setting, fill washer with hot water and add a small amount of mild detergent or dishwashing liquid. Place old towels or a pair of jeans (to help with the felting process) and the pot holders in washer, and agitate until they are the correct size and the individual stitches are no longer visible. Check frequently (approximately every minute). Once felted, remove from washer, rinse in hot water, and pat dry in a towel to remove excess water. Do not wring. Block pot holders to size; let dry.

Green Pot Holder Embellishment

Row 1: Single crochet around edge with Leaf Green, making 3 single crochets in each corner to maintain square shaping.

Row 2: Single crochet around edge with Rich Red.

Row 3: Single crochet around edge with Old Gold.

With Old Gold, crochet a chain loop (about 3" [7.5cm] long, before folding in half) in 1 corner of pot holder. With Old Gold, work a leaf stitch in 2 opposite corners. With Rich Red, work a leaf stitch in remaining corners. Weave in loose ends.

Red Pot Holder Embellishment

Row 1: Single crochet around edge with Rich Red, making 3 single crochets in each corner to maintain shaping.

Row 2: Single crochet around edge with Old Gold.

Row 3: Single crochet around edge with Leaf Green.

With Leaf Green, crochet a chain loop (about 3" [7.5cm] long, before folding in half) in 1 corner of pot holder. With Old Gold and Leaf Green, work several leaf stitches in a random pattern over pot holder. Weave in loose ends.

Gold Pot Holder Embellishment

Row 1: Single crochet around edge with Old Gold, making 3 single crochets in each corner to maintain shaping.

Row 2: Single crochet around edge with Leaf Green.

Row 3: Single crochet around edge with Rich Red.

With Rich Red, crochet a chain loop (about 3" [7.5cm] long, before folding in half) in 1 corner of pot holder. With Rich Red, work 2 leaf stitches across from each other at the center. With Leaf Green, work 2 leaf stitches across from each other in between Rich Red leaves. Weave in loose ends.

Wacky Kids' Crafts

"Gone Batty" Jewelry

Guests at your holiday haunting will go batty over this quick-and-fun project. Have your kids make it as a gift for a spooktacular teacher!

What You'll Need

- Markers: black fine-tip permanent; black chisel-tip permanent; silver metallic fine-point (1mm)
- 2×4-inch black foam sheeting
- Scissors
- 1/16-inch paper punch
- Medium oval wood piece
- Foam glue
- 2 wiggle eyes, 5mm each
- 50 inches decorative furry yarn
- Tape measure
- Orange pony beads, 9×6mm
- Black embroidery floss
- Embroidery needle

1 Trace bat pattern on page 76 onto foam with black fine-tip marker, and cut out.

2 Use paper punch to make a hole approximately 1/8 inch in from neck edge of bat. Punch hole in oval wood piece to match hole in bat. Paint oval using chisel-tip marker. Let dry. Glue oval to center of bat, matching holes. Glue on wiggle eyes, and use silver marker to draw mouth and vampire teeth.

3 Cut 36 inches of yarn. String and tie pony beads onto yarn, spacing beads 1½ to 2½ inches apart. Tie yarn ends together at back. Fold necklace in half to find middle of front. Tie an overhand knot at center front of necklace.

4 Using embroidery needle and floss, thread floss through hole punched in bat body. Bring needle through knot at center front of necklace. Knot floss ends together, leaving enough room for bat to hang 1½ inches below knot.

5 Determine bracelet size by measuring wrist then multiplying by 3. Cut yarn to determined length and add pony beads, knotting them in place as with necklace. Wrap around wrist and tie yarn ends using an overhand knot. Trim yarn ends.

Pattern is 100%.

Trick-or-Treat Bag

Treats taste better when they are tricked out of this boo-tiful bag.

What You'll Need

- Brown grocery bag (6½×10-inch base, at least 12 inches high)
- Ruler
- Scissors: pinking, regular
- Shiny paper: 9-inch square white, 9-inch square orange, 2×3 inches yellow, 2-inch square green, 2×3 inches black
- Pencil
- Black permanent felt-tipped marker
- 1½×18 inches white posterboard
- Glue stick
- 52 inches Halloween print ribbon, 1½ inch wide
- Low-temp glue gun, glue sticks

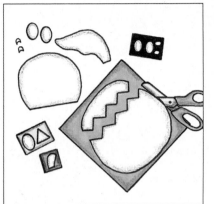

2 Using patterns on page 78, trace and cut the following: ghost head, arm, and eye crescents and jack-o'-lantern eyes from white paper; jack-o'-lantern and top from orange paper; jack-o'-lantern nose and mouth from yellow paper; stem from green paper; and jack-o'-lantern pupils and ghost eyes from black paper.

3 Referring to photo, position parts on worktable in the following order: ghost head, arm, jack-o'-lantern top, stem, head, eyes and pupils, nose, mouth, and ghost eyes and eye crescents. Use glue stick to assemble. Using a black marker, draw eyebrows and mouth on ghost and eyebrows on pumpkin (see finished photograph). Use glue stick to attach entire jack-o'-lantern/ghost piece to the front of the bag.

1 Use ruler to measure grocery bag to 12 inches high. Cut along line with pinking shears.

4 To make handle, use a glue gun (set on low) to glue 1 inch of poster-board strip to the top outside middle of the short side of the bag. Repeat on other side of bag with other end of poster-board strip. Glue one end of ribbon to bottom middle of bag, spot gluing as you go up side of bag, across poster-board strip, down other side, and across middle of bottom until overlapping other end. Fill the bag with treats!

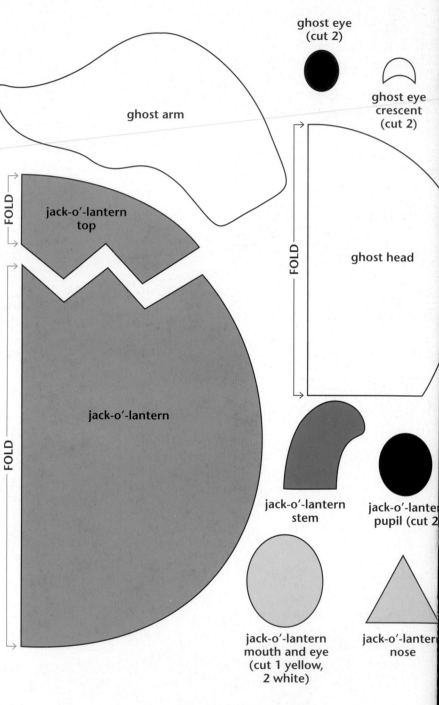

ghost arm

ghost eye (cut 2)

ghost eye crescent (cut 2)

FOLD

jack-o'-lantern top

FOLD

ghost head

FOLD

jack-o'-lantern

jack-o'-lantern stem

jack-o'-lantern pupil (cut 2)

jack-o'-lantern mouth and eye (cut 1 yellow, 2 white)

jack-o'-lantern nose

Enlarge patterns 166%.

Marvelous Masks

What You'll Need

Feather mask

- 5-inch squares tissue paper: blue, red, yellow, green
- 4×8 inches white posterboard
- Glue stick
- Pencil, scissors
- Low-temp glue gun, glue sticks
- 37 inches yellow baby rickrack
- Hole punch
- 14 inches white elastic cord, ¼ inch wide
- 6 matching feathers

Spider mask

- 4×8 inches orange posterboard
- Pencil, scissors
- Shiny black dimensional paint
- Hole punch
- 14 inches white elastic cord, ¼ inch wide
- Black poms: two 1 inch, two ¾ inch
- 4 wiggle eyes, 7mm each
- Tweezers
- 2 black chenille stems
- Low-temp glue gun, glue sticks
- Black yarn: 22 inches; 8 inches (cut in half)

Feather Mask Instructions

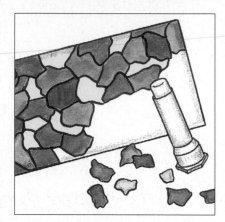

1 Rip tissue paper into irregular ½-inch to 1¼-inch pieces. Apply glue stick to posterboard. Attach ripped pieces, overlapping edges and randomly placing colors until entire posterboard is covered. Turn over posterboard. Trace mask outline and eye holes onto posterboard using pattern from page 82. Cut on lines. Turn right side up.

2 Use glue gun (on low) for the following: glue five inches of rickrack, a few inches at a time, around each eye hole. Also, glue 27-inch length of rickrack around outside edge of mask. Punch hole on each side of mask where indicated on pattern. Insert ends of elastic through holes, and tie knots at back of mask—adjust as needed to fit your head. Spot glue elastic knots to hold.

3 Glue ends of 3 feather to back top of mask or each side.

81

Spider Mask Instructions

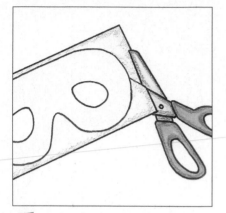

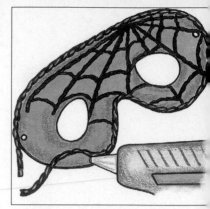

1 Trace mask outline and eye holes onto back side of orange posterboard. Cut on lines. Punch holes on sides where indicated.

2 Lightly draw pencil web guidelines on front of mask according to spider pattern. Squeeze dimensional paint on web lines; let dry.

3 Glue together 1-inch and ¾-inch black poms for spider's head and body. Use tweezers to glue 2 wiggle eyes to front of head. For legs, stack and glue middles of four 3-inch lengths of chenille stems. Glue body to top of leg stack. Bend legs down ½ inch on end of each leg. Bend out a ¼ inch on end for foot. Slightly flatten legs. Repeat procedure to make another spider but do not flatten legs.

4 Leaving 2 inches unglued, begin gluing 22-inch length of yarn about ½ inch above left hole punch, continuing all the way around outside of mask. Glue first spider to top right of mask. Glue dangling end of yarn between second spider's head and body pom. Glue 4-inch lengths of yarn around eye holes. Attach elastic cord as explained in step 2 of the feather mask directions.

Enlarge pattern 143%.

Halloween Mobile

This Halloween mobile hangs from above.
It's as spooky as a cobweb in the corner!

What You'll Need

- Foam sheet: 5×5 inches yellow; 3×6 inches orange; 3×7 inches white; 5×5 inches black

- Pencil

- Scissors

- Hole punch

- Fine-point opaque paint markers: black, brown

- Wiggle eyes: eighteen 12mm; four 5mm

- Craft glue

- 58-inch length of black satin ribbon, ⅛-inch wide

- Ruler

- ¼-inch black pom

1 Using the patterns on page 84, trace and cut the following shapes from foam: moon from yellow; 2 pumpkins from orange; 2 skulls from white; bat, cat head, and 2 cat paws from black. Use hole punch to make holes in the foam shapes in the places indicated on the patterns.

2 Decorate both sides of the pumpkins by drawing lines with the brown marker and faces with the black marker; let dry. Draw faces on both sides of the skulls with the black marker; let dry. Glue two 5mm eyes on both sides of the bat. Glue two 12mm eyes on both sides of the pumpkins and skulls.

cat paw

cat head

3 Cut a 12-inch length of ribbon. Insert an end of the ribbon 1½ inches into the single hole at the top of the moon. Tie a double knot in the ribbon to securely attach it to the moon. Trim the short end of the ribbon close to the knot. Position and glue the cat head on the back upper side of the moon. Position and glue the cat paws on the front of the moon, with the right paw covering the ribbon hanger. Glue the black pom nose on the cat head so that it slightly overlaps the edge of the moon, and glue two 12mm eyes to the cat head.

4 Cut the remaining ribbon into the following lengths, and use double knots to tie one end of each length to a foam shape and the other end to a hole at the bottom of the moon: a 6-inch length for a pumpkin; a 9-inch length for a skull; a 13-inch length for the bat; an 11-inch length for a pumpkin; a 7-inch length for a skull. Trim the ends of each length of ribbon close to the knots.

Enlarge patterns 155%.

skull

bat

moon

pumpkin

pumpkin

84

Spooky Skeleton

Your face will turn white with fright when you spy this spine-chilling sight!

What You'll Need
- 7 white bump chenille stems
- Scissors

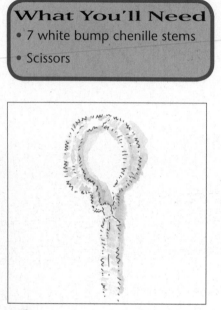

1 Cut a 2-bump section from a chenille stem for the spine. To make the skull, cut 2 bumps and twist the thin part between the bumps together, hiding them in the bumps to create a long bump. Bend the long bump into a circle. Twist the thin ends onto the spine.

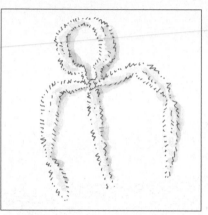

2 Find the middle of a stem and twist it to the spine just under the skull. Bend this stem to form shoulders and arms; cut stems after each shoulder bump and remove most of thin pieces. Twist thin pieces together for elbow joints. Repeat after next bump for wrists.

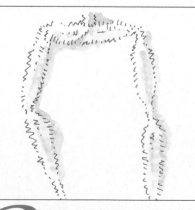

3 Cut a 1-bump piece, and twist it to the bottom of the spine for the skeleton's hips. Cut another stem in half, and twist each piece to one side of hip bone. Bend and twist each leg between bumps to create knees.

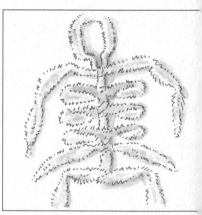

4 To make the rib cage, cut four 2-bump pieces and twist them onto the spine. Bend each rib around the spine toward the front of the skeleton.

5 Cut the remaining stem into 4 bumps, and bend each bump in half. Twist one to each arm and leg to create hands and feet.

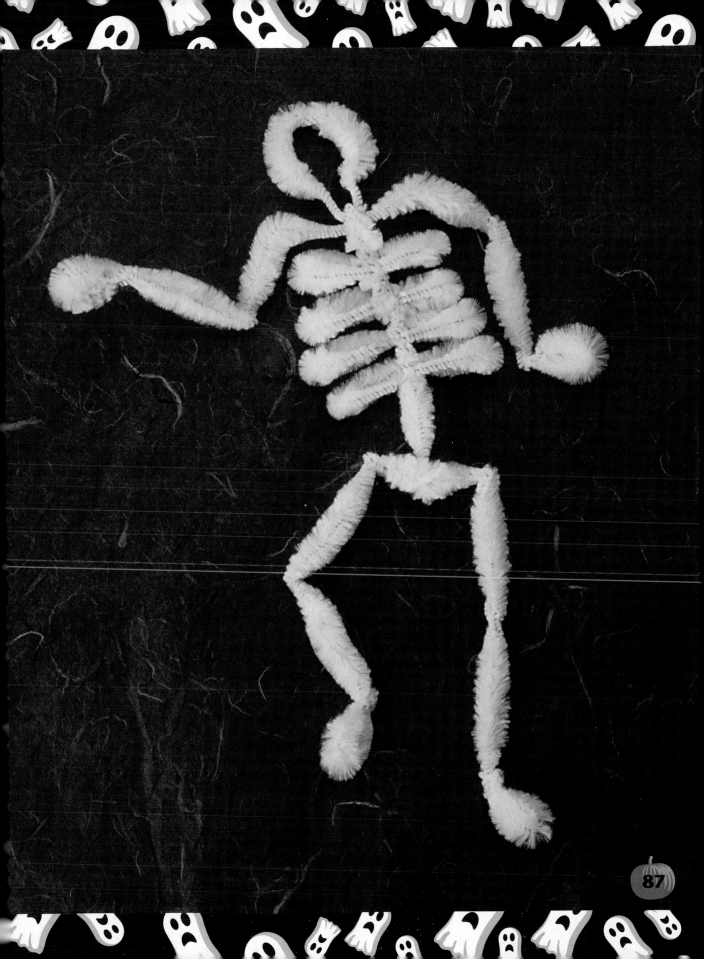

Rockin' Spider

Your parents might shriek in horror when they see your new pet, but at least they won't yell at you to feed it!

What You'll Need

- Smooth, round rock
- Paintbrush
- Acrylic paint: black, pink dimensional
- Acrylic gloss medium (optional)
- Scissors
- 2 black chenille stems
- Wax paper or newspaper
- Low-temp glue gun, glue sticks
- Craft glue
- 2 wiggle eyes

1 Wash and dry rock. Paint the rock with 2 coats of black paint. Let paint dry between coats. Paint a final coat of acrylic gloss medium, if desired.

2 Cut the chenille stems in half so you have four 6-inch pieces. Shape the ends of each piece to make arched legs. Flatten out the middle of the stems so the rock will fit on top of the stems.

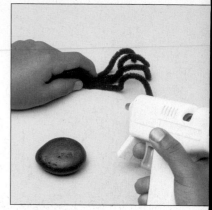

3 Cover the work surface with wax paper or newspaper. Hold the 4 bent stems together. Apply a generous amount of glue to the flat center area. Put the rock on top of the glue, holding it down until the glue sets.

4 Paint a smile on the spider with pink paint. Using craft glue, attach wiggle eyes to the front of the spider.

Spooky Tic-Tac-Toe

Frighten a friend into playing a game of spooky tic-tac-toe.
Your friend will fear more than just losing.

What You'll Need

- Magnetic sheeting: black 5×5-inch piece; orange and white 1½×7½-inch pieces
- Pencil
- Scissors: regular, manicure
- Fine-point opaque paint markers: black, brown
- 20 inches green satin ribbon, ⅛ inch wide
- Ruler
- Craft glue

1 Using the patterns on page 92, trace and cut 5 pumpkins from the orange magnetic sheeting and 5 ghosts from the white magnetic sheeting. When cutting the magnetic sheeting, use regular scissors most of the time, and use small manicure scissors for small curves.

2 Draw the stem and lines on the pumpkins with the brown marker; let dry. Draw faces on the pumpkins with the black marker; let dry.

3 Draw eyes and mouths on the ghosts with the black marker; let dry.

4 Cut the ribbon into four 5-inch lengths. Glue 4 lengths of ribbon to the black magnetic sheeting to make a tic-tac-toe grid.

Patterns are 100%.

Finger Foods

Bloody Monster Claws

5 small red potatoes, scrubbed and cut into 4 slices lengthwise, about ¼ inch thick
¼ cup olive oil
Paprika
Salt and black pepper
Varieties of ketchup (purple, green, or red)

1 Preheat oven to 425°F.

2 Cut 2 wedges from end of each potato slice to resemble claw. Place oil in 15×10×1-inch jelly-roll pan; tilt to coat bottom evenly. Place potato slices evenly in prepared pan. Sprinkle slices with paprika; turn to coat with oil and sprinkle with paprika.

3 Bake 5 minutes. Turn slices; bake 4 minutes or just until fork tender. Sprinkle with salt and pepper. Serve with ketchups. Makes 20 claws

Trick or Treats

12 cups popcorn

1 pound bacon, crisp-cooked and broken into 1-inch pieces

1 can (12 ounces) mixed nuts, toasted*

½ cup sunflower seeds, toasted**

4 tablespoons butter or margarine, melted

3 tablespoons grated Parmesan cheese

*To toast mixed nuts, spread in single layer on baking sheet. Bake in preheated 350°F oven 5 to 7 minutes or until fragrant, stirring occasionally.

**To toast seeds, place in single layer on baking sheet. Bake at 350°F 7 to 10 minutes or until golden brown, stirring occasionally. Cool completely.

1 Combine popcorn, bacon, nuts, and sunflower seeds in large bowl.

2 Drizzle mixture with butter. Sprinkle with cheese; toss. Serve warm.

Makes 12 (1-cup) servings

Gushing Goo Rolls

12 corn tortillas

2 tablespoons olive oil

1 envelope (1¼ ounces) taco seasoning mix

12 mozzarella-cheddar swirled cheese sticks

Nonstick cooking spray

Chopped cilantro (optional)

1 Preheat oven to 475°F. Line baking sheet with foil.

2 Place one tortilla on prepared baking sheet. Brush one side of tortilla with oil; sprinkle with 1 teaspoon taco seasoning. Top with one cheese stick; roll up tightly. Lay seam side down on prepared baking sheet. Spray top with cooking spray. Repeat with remaining tortillas.

3 Bake 6 minutes or until cheese begins to melt. Remove from oven and let stand 3 minutes to allow cheese to set slightly. Sprinkle with chopped cilantro.

Makes 12 rolls

Haunted Tip

Before assembling rolls, cover tortillas with foil and warm briefly in the oven to make them more pliable.

Crispy Goblin Chips

¼ cup sugar
1 teaspoon ground cinnamon
1 large sweet potato, cut into ¹⁄₁₆-inch slices
Vegetable oil

1 Combine sugar and cinnamon in small bowl; set aside. Cut out Halloween shapes using cookie cutters.

2 Place oil in large deep skillet, filling about half full. Heat oil to 350°F on deep-fry thermometer. Place potatoes in hot oil in single layer; fry 2 to 3 minutes or until crispy. Remove from oil; drain on paper towels. Sprinkle with cinnamon-sugar mixture. Repeat with remaining potatoes. Makes 25 to 30 chips

Sticks 'n' Stones

4 cups caramel popcorn
4 cups unseasoned croutons
¾ cup sesame sticks
¾ cup toasted pumpkin or sunflower seeds*
¼ cup (½ stick) butter, melted
1 package (1 ounce) dry ranch-style salad dressing mix

*To toast seeds, place in single layer on baking sheet. Bake at 350°F 7 to 10 minutes or until golden brown, stirring occasionally. Cool completely.

1 Preheat oven to 300°F.

2 Combine caramel popcorn, croutons, sesame sticks, and pumpkin seeds on ungreased 15×10×1-inch jelly-roll pan. Drizzle with butter and sprinkle with dressing mix. Toss to coat.

3 Bake 15 minutes, stirring occasionally. Cool 10 minutes on pan. Turn out onto paper towels; cool completely. Makes 10 cups

98

See photo on page 41.

Crispy Goblin Chips

Dinosaur Eggs

6 eggs

2 teaspoons salt

4 tablespoons soy sauce

2 tablespoons unsulphured molasses

8 tea bags (preferably black tea)

⅓ cup mayonnaise

2 tablespoons finely minced red bell pepper

1 cup salsa

Salt and ground black pepper

Cracked black pepper (optional)

1 Cover eggs with 1 inch of cold water in large saucepan; bring to a boil. Remove from heat and let stand, covered, 10 minutes. Drain and refill saucepan with cold water; let stand 5 minutes.

2 Gently tap shells with back of spoon until each shell is crackled, but not falling off. Return eggs to saucepan. Cover with cold water; add salt, soy sauce, molasses, and tea bags. Bring to a boil, reduce heat, and let eggs simmer 30 minutes. Remove saucepan from heat; let eggs stand in liquid, uncovered, until cool. Drain. Chill overnight.

3 Peel eggs. Trim base of each egg to stand upright. Slice eggs lengthwise and scoop out yolks. Mix yolks with mayonnaise, bell pepper, salt, and ground black pepper in small bowl.

4 Spoon yolk mixture back into egg whites; level with knife. Put egg halves back together. Cover plate evenly with salsa; set eggs upright on plate. Sprinkle with cracked black pepper.   Makes 12 servings

Dragon Breath

2 packages (about 10 ounces each) refrigerated garlic breadstick dough
   Minced garlic
1 to 2 tablespoons kosher salt
½ cup mayonnaise
3 tablespoons spicy yellow mustard
1 teaspoon dry mustard
1 teaspoon sugar
1 teaspoon lemon juice
   Black olives, halved
   Red bell pepper, cut into 1-inch strips

1 Preheat oven to 375°F. Unroll dough onto large ungreased baking sheet.

2 Roll 1 piece of breadstick dough for body of dragon into 12-inch log. Place on baking sheet and twist bottom of dough under to form tail. Make small cut at top and bottom of dough for mouth and tail, using scissors or small knife. Flatten 1 piece of breadstick dough slightly and cut in half crosswise to form 2 rectangles. Make small cut on one side of rectangle for wing; press edges onto right side of body. Repeat with second rectangle; press edges onto left side of body. Sprinkle dragons with garlic and kosher salt. Repeat with remaining dough.

3 Bake 13 to 18 minutes or until golden brown.

4 Press olive onto each dragon for eye and pepper strip for tongue. Combine mayonnaise, yellow mustard, dry mustard, sugar, and lemon juice in small bowl. Serve with dragons as dipping sauce.   Makes 10 servings

Magic Wands

1 cup semisweet chocolate chips

12 pretzel rods

3 squares (1 ounce each) white chocolate

Orange food coloring

Assorted sprinkles

1 Line baking sheet with waxed paper.

2 Melt semisweet chocolate in top of double boiler over hot, not boiling, water. Remove from heat. Dip pretzel rods into chocolate, spooning chocolate over pretzels to coat about ¾ of each pretzel. Place on prepared baking sheet. Refrigerate until chocolate is set.

3 Melt white chocolate in top of clean double boiler over hot, not boiling, water. Stir in food coloring until desired shade of orange is reached. Remove from heat. Dip coated pretzels quickly into colored chocolate to coat about ¼ of each pretzel. Place pretzels on prepared baking sheet; immediately top with sprinkles. Refrigerate until chocolate is set.   Makes 12 wands

Fish Biters

24 giant goldfish-shaped crackers

12 slices pepperoni, halved

12 Monterey Jack cheese cubes, halved

24 small black olive slices

24 fresh parsley leaves

1 Preheat oven to 425°F. Coat baking sheet with nonstick cooking spray.

2 Place crackers on prepared baking sheet. Place 2 pepperoni halves on tail ends. Place cheese cube half in center of each fish.

3 Bake 3 minutes or until cheese is melted. Remove from oven; top with olive slices to resemble eyes. Lift up olive slices slightly and place parsley leaves behind them to resemble fins. Press down olives to adhere. Serve warm.

Makes 24 crackers

Haunted Tip

Fish Biters may be assembled up to 2 hours in advance. Complete steps 1 and 2. Cover with a sheet of plastic wrap or foil and refrigerate until ready to bake.

Stuffed Bundles

1 package (10 ounces) refrigerated pizza dough
2 ounces ham, chopped
½ cup (2 ounces) shredded sharp Cheddar cheese

1 Preheat oven to 425°F. Coat nonstick 12-cup muffin pan with nonstick cooking spray.

2 Unroll dough on flat surface; cut into 12 pieces (4×3-inch rectangles). Divide ham and cheese between dough rectangles. Bring corners of dough together, pinching to seal. Place, smooth side up, in prepared muffin cups.

3 Bake 10 to 12 minutes or until golden brown.

Makes 12 servings

Guacamole

2 large avocados
¼ cup chopped tomato
2 tablespoons fresh lime juice or lemon juice
2 tablespoons minced onion
½ teaspoon salt
¼ teaspoon hot pepper sauce
   Black pepper

1 Place avocados in medium bowl; mash coarsely with fork. Stir in tomato, lime juice, onion, salt, hot pepper sauce, and black pepper; mix well.

2 Serve immediately.

Makes 2 cups

See photo on page 33.

Stuffed Bundles

Freaky Fondue

4 (10-inch) spinach- or tomato-flavored flour tortillas
   Nonstick cooking spray
1 cup canned cheese dip, Cheddar cheese sauce, or salsa con queso
8 small carrots, peeled
8 almond slices
1 small jicama, peeled
1 cup cauliflower
1 tablespoon milk
1 tablespoon salsa

1 For tortilla hands, preheat oven to 325°F. Cut tortillas in half. Use small knife to cut each tortilla half into shape of small hand; discard trimmings.

2 Place tortilla cutouts on ungreased baking sheet. To create curved hands, drape cutouts over small bowls or custard cups. Spray both sides of cutouts with cooking spray. Bake 10 minutes or until lightly browned.

3 For carrot fingers, cut notch in narrow end for nail bed. Use small dab of cheese dip to "glue" almond slice onto nail bed to resemble fingernail. For jicama bones, cut jicama into ¼-inch slices; cut rectangle from each slice. Trim ends of rectangles with small knife to resemble bones. Arrange cauliflower "brains," tortilla hands, carrot fingers, and jicama bones on large platter.

4 Stir milk into remaining cheese dip in microwavable serving bowl until blended. Microwave on HIGH 15 seconds or until heated through. Swirl salsa on top. Place warm dip in center of platter; serve immediately.

Makes 8 to 10 servings

Merlin's Magic Mix

6 cups unbuttered popcorn, lightly salted

1 cup pretzel nuggets

1 cup slivered almonds, toasted and lightly salted*

¼ cup (½ stick) butter

¼ cup light corn syrup

¾ cup firmly packed light brown sugar

⅓ cup red cinnamon candies

1 cup mini candy-coated chocolate pieces

¾ cup sweetened dried cranberries

*To toast almonds, spread in single layer on baking sheet. Bake in preheated 350°F oven 5 to 7 minutes or until fragrant, stirring occasionally.

1 Preheat oven to 250°F. Lightly grease 2 large baking pans; set aside. Place popped popcorn in large bowl. Add pretzel nuggets and almonds; set aside.

2 Stir butter and corn syrup in medium saucepan over low heat until melted. Add brown sugar; cook and stir until sugar is melted and mixture comes to a boil. Boil 5 minutes, stirring frequently. Remove from heat; add cinnamon candies, stirring until melted. Stir sugar mixture into popcorn mixture with lightly greased spatula until evenly coated. Spread popcorn mixture in even layer in prepared pans.

3 Bake 10 to 15 minutes, stirring every 5 minutes with lightly greased spoon to separate popcorn. Cool completely in pans on wire racks. Combine popcorn mixture, candy pieces, and cranberries in large bowl. Store in tightly covered container.   Makes about 8 cups

Smashed Thumbsticks
with Oily Dipping Sauce

1 package (about 11 ounces) refrigerated breadstick dough

12 sun-dried tomatoes, cut in half crosswise, or jumbo pitted green olives, halved lengthwise

½ cup plus 2 tablespoons olive oil, divided

Dried dill or rosemary

2 tablespoons balsamic vinegar

1 teaspoon dried basil

½ teaspoon salt

¼ teaspoon black pepper

1 Preheat oven to 375°F.

2 Unroll breadstick dough; separate into strips and cut in half crosswise. Place on 2 ungreased baking sheets. Place tomato half about ⅛ inch from top of each strip; press down firmly. Shape ends to round out tip of thumb. Gently press down on dough with flat side of knife to resemble knuckles. Brush breadsticks with 2 tablespoons olive oil; sprinkle with dill.

3 Bake 10 minutes or until light golden brown.

4 Meanwhile, combine ½ cup olive oil, balsamic vinegar, basil, salt, and pepper in small bowl; whisk until well blended. Serve with thumbsticks.

Makes 12 servings

Grubs and Bugs

3 cans (8 ounces each) refrigerated crescent roll dough
2 packages (16 ounces each) cocktail franks (58 franks)
1 bag (about 15 ounces) thin pretzel sticks

1 Preheat oven to 375°F. Grease 2 baking sheets.

2 Unroll dough; separate along perforated lines into 24 triangles. (Spray hands with nonstick cooking spray as necessary to prevent dough from sticking to them.) Cut one piece of dough with serrated knife into three smaller triangles by cutting through corner opposite widest side. Repeat with nine additional pieces of dough. Slice remaining 14 pieces of dough in half.

3 For Grubs, place 1 cocktail frank on longest side of 1 large triangle; fold sides over ends of frank; roll up to opposite point, pinching dough as necessary to completely cover frank. Place seam side down on prepared baking sheet. Repeat with remaining large triangles. Bake 11 to 15 minutes or until deep golden brown. Immediately remove from baking sheet to wire rack; cool completely.

4 For Bugs, place 1 cocktail frank on shortest side of 1 small triangle; roll to opposite point. Poke 3 pretzel pieces into dough along each side to make legs with points facing down. Place seam side down on prepared baking sheet. Repeat with remaining small triangles and franks. Bake 11 to 15 minutes or until deep golden brown. Immediately remove from baking sheet to wire rack; cool completely.

Makes 28 servings

Creepy Cheese Curls

4 green onions
1½ cups (6 ounces) shredded mozzarella cheese*
½ cup (2 ounces) grated Parmesan cheese
1 teaspoon chili powder
1 teaspoon black pepper
Nonstick cooking spray

*Shred cheese using largest holes on box grater. If purchasing shredded cheese, look for "chef-style" cheese, which is grated into larger than usual pieces.

1 Cut single slit in each green onion by running tip of paring knife down the length of each green top once. Slice green tips crosswise into thin ribbons. Toss green onions, mozzarella cheese, Parmesan cheese, chili powder, and pepper in medium bowl.

2 Coat medium skillet with cooking spray; heat over medium-high heat. Spoon about ½ to 1 tablespoon cheese mixture into skillet to make 2-inch circle. Cook 1 to 1½ minutes until cheese melts and turns golden brown. Immediately remove from pan with thin metal spatula; cool completely on parchment-lined baking sheet. Repeat with remaining cheese mixture.

3 Store in airtight container until ready to serve.   Makes 8 servings

Haunted Tip

Creepy Cheese Curls are extremely hot and pliable when first removed from the skillet. The curls will become crisp and chewy as they cool. To easily mold them, drape over a rolling pin instead of cooling on a baking sheet.

Jack-o'-Lantern Snacks

1 package (8 ounces) cream cheese, softened
   Red and yellow food coloring
8 large slices dark pumpernickel bread
1 small green bell pepper
   Sliced Genoa salami

1 Place cream cheese in small bowl. Add 8 drops red and 6 drops yellow food coloring to turn cream cheese orange. Mix well and adjust color as desired.

2 Toast bread; cool completely. Cut round shape from each slice of toast leaving "stem" on top, using large pumpkin cookie cutter or metal 1-cup measure.

3 Spread cream cheese over toast to edges. Cut "stems" from pepper and place over stems on toast. Cut triangle eyes and mouth with several teeth from sliced salami. Arrange over each pumpkin toast.

Makes 8 servings

Lake of Fire

½ cup sour cream

½ cup mayonnaise

4 ounces cream cheese

1 bottle (12 ounces) roasted red peppers, drained

1 medium clove garlic, minced

1 teaspoon salt

¾ teaspoon ground cumin

⅓ cup lime juice

¼ teaspoon ground red pepper (optional)

Tortilla chips, broccoli, cucumber slices, and bell pepper strips

1 In a food processor, combine sour cream, mayonnaise, cream cheese, roasted red peppers, garlic, salt, cumin, lime juice, and ground red pepper, if desired. Process until smooth. Refrigerate overnight or up to 48 hours.

2 Serve with tortilla chips, broccoli, cucumber, and bell pepper strips.

Makes 12 servings

Shrunken Dunkin' Skulls

2 tablespoons cornmeal

1 package (14 ounces) refrigerated pizza crust dough

2 cloves garlic, halved

2 teaspoons dried basil

1 teaspoon dried oregano

Salt (optional)

2 tablespoons olive oil

2 tablespoons grated Parmesan cheese

1 cup marinara sauce, warmed

1 cup ranch dressing

1 Preheat oven to 400°F. Spray baking sheet with nonstick cooking spray; sprinkle evenly with cornmeal. Set aside.

2 Unroll pizza dough onto cutting board. Rub with garlic; sprinkle evenly with basil and oregano. Cut out 12 circles, using 2½-inch biscuit cutter; place on baking sheet. Stretch into oval shapes. Use leftover dough scraps for eyes, noses, and mouths. Sprinkle with salt, if desired.

3 Bake 10 minutes or until golden brown. Brush with olive oil and sprinkle with cheese. Serve with marinara sauce and ranch dressing.   Makes 12 skulls

Monster Munch

6 squares (2 ounces each) almond bark, divided

1½ cups pretzel sticks

Orange food coloring (optional)

2 cups graham cereal

¾ cup orange and brown candy-coated chocolate pieces

¾ cup mini marshmallows

½ cup chocolate sprinkles

Microwave Directions

1 Place 1½ squares almond bark in small microwavable bowl. Microwave on MEDIUM (50%) 1 minute; stir. Repeat as necessary, stirring at 15-second intervals until completely melted.

2 Place pretzel sticks in large bowl. Add melted almond bark; stir until all pieces are coated evenly. Spread coated pretzel sticks out on waxed paper, separating individual pieces; let set.

3 Place remaining 4½ squares almond bark in medium microwavable bowl. Microwave on MEDIUM (50%) 1 minute; stir. Repeat as necessary, stirring at 15-second intervals until completely melted. Stir in food coloring, if desired, until almond bark is bright orange.

4 Place cereal in large bowl. Add half of orange-colored almond bark and stir until cereal is coated evenly. Add chocolate pieces, marshmallows, and remaining almond bark; stir until mix is coated evenly. Stir in pretzel sticks.

5 Break mix into small clusters and spread out on waxed paper. Sprinkle clusters with chocolate sprinkles; let stand until set.   Makes about 5 cups

Quicksand

¾ cup creamy peanut butter

5 ounces cream cheese, softened

1 cup pineapple preserves

⅓ cup milk

1 teaspoon Worcestershire sauce

Dash hot pepper sauce (optional)

1 can (7 ounces) refrigerated breadstick dough (6 breadsticks)

5 crackers, crushed

Carrots, celery, and/or apple slices (optional)

1 Combine peanut butter and cream cheese in large bowl until well blended. Stir in preserves, milk, Worcestershire sauce, and hot pepper sauce, if desired. Transfer to serving bowl; cover with plastic wrap. Refrigerate until ready to serve.

2 Preheat oven to 375°F. Cut each breadstick in half crosswise; place on ungreased baking sheet. Make 3 slits in one short end of each breadstick half to resemble fingers. Cut small piece of dough from other short end; press dough piece into hand to resemble thumb. Bake 8 to 10 minutes or until golden brown.

3 Just before serving, sprinkle dip with cracker crumbs. Serve with breadstick hands, carrots, celery, and apples, if desired.   Makes 12 to 16 servings

Monster Mash Spread

1 package (8 ounces) cream cheese, softened
2 cups (8 ounces) shredded Monterey Jack cheese with jalapeño peppers
½ cup chopped green bell pepper
¼ cup finely chopped green onions
   Green Onion Curls (recipe follows)
   Assorted crackers

1 Line 8- or 9-inch round cake pan with foil. Spray with nonstick cooking spray; set aside.

2 Combine cream cheese, Monterey Jack cheese, bell pepper, and chopped green onions in medium bowl; mix well. Spoon into prepared pan; press mixture evenly into pan. Cover; refrigerate 1 to 2 hours or overnight.

3 To serve, invert pan onto large platter or serving tray. Remove pan and discard foil. Garnish with Green Onion Curls. Serve with crackers.

Makes 2 cups

Green Onion Curls

3 to 4 green onions (tops only)

1 Cut each green onion lengthwise into long, narrow strips, using scissors or small knife. Place strips in bowl of ice water; refrigerate until curled, about 2 hours or overnight.

Makes 20 to 30 curls

Hot Molten Blobs

1 package (12 ounces) buttermilk biscuit dough

2 tablespoons mayonnaise

1 tablespoon plus 1½ teaspoons honey mustard

1 thick slice ham, cut into 10 (¼-inch) cubes

1 block Cheddar cheese, cut into 30 (¼-inch) cubes

1 Preheat oven to 400°F. Spray 10 standard (2½-inch) muffin cups with nonstick cooking spray. Line center rack of oven with foil.

2 Separate dough into individual biscuits; place 1 biscuit in each prepared muffin cup. Combine mayonnaise and mustard in small bowl; stir until well blended.

3 Press down with thumbs to make deep indentation in each biscuit. Spoon about 1 teaspoon mayonnaise mixture into each biscuit. Top with 1 ham cube and 3 cheese cubes.

4 Bake about 12 minutes or until biscuits are golden, slightly puffed and overflowing with cheese. Let stand 3 minutes before removing from pan. Serve warm. _Makes 10 blobs_

Haunted Tip

Serve blobs with scrambled eggs and orange juice for a bewitching breakfast.

Creepy Hands

8 cups popcorn
1 cup pumpkin seeds, cleaned and patted dry
⅓ cup butter or margarine, melted
1 tablespoon Worcestershire sauce
½ teaspoon garlic salt
½ teaspoon seasoned salt
   Candy corn

1 Preheat oven to 300°F. Place popcorn in single layer in 15×10×1-inch jelly-roll pan; sprinkle pumpkin seeds evenly over top.

2 Combine butter, Worcestershire sauce, garlic salt, and seasoned salt in small bowl; mix well. Pour over popcorn; toss lightly to evenly coat.

3 Bake 30 minutes, stirring after 15 minutes. Cool completely in pan on wire rack.

4 Place candy corn in each finger of 6 clear industrial food-safe gloves for fingernails. Pack gloves with popcorn mixture. Close gloves at wrists; tie with ribbons. Place spider ring on one finger of each glove hand.   Makes 6 servings

Cheesy Bat Biscuits

1 can (16 ounces) jumbo buttermilk biscuit dough

3 tablespoons butter, melted and divided

¼ cup grated Parmesan cheese

1 teaspoon dried parsley

1 teaspoon dried basil

1 Preheat oven to 350°F.

2 Separate biscuits; flatten each into shape just large enough to fit 3-inch bat cookie cutter. Cut out bat shape; discard scraps. Place biscuits on baking sheet. Lightly score biscuits to outline bat wings; poke holes with toothpick for eyes. Brush biscuits with 1 tablespoon butter. Bake 7 minutes.

3 Meanwhile, combine cheese, remaining 2 tablespoons butter, parsley, and basil in small bowl.

4 Turn biscuits on end and split into halves with forks. Spread 1 teaspoon cheese mixture on bottom half of each biscuit; replace biscuit top. Bake 3 minutes or until biscuits are golden brown.   Makes 8 servings

Kooky Entrées

Bat & Spook Pizzas

4 (6-inch) Italian bread shells
⅔ cup pizza or pasta sauce
1 package (3½ ounces) pepperoni slices
4 slices (1 ounce each) mozzarella cheese

1 Preheat oven to 375°F.

2 Place bread shells on ungreased baking sheet. Spread pizza sauce evenly on bread shells; top evenly with pepperoni slices. Cut out ghost and bat shapes from cheese slices with cookie cutters; place on pizza sauce.

3 Bake 10 to 12 minutes or until cheese is melted.   Makes 4 servings

Pumpkin Pizzas

Spread bread shells with pizza sauce as directed. Omit pepperoni. Substitute process American cheese slices for mozzarella; cut into triangles. Place cheese triangles on pizza sauce to make jack-o'-lantern faces. Place ¼ cup broccoli florets for eyes and 2 cherry tomatoes, halved, for noses. Bake as directed.

Spaghetti and Eyeballs

1 pound ground beef
½ cup bread crumbs
⅓ cup milk
1 egg
2 tablespoons finely chopped onion
½ teaspoon garlic salt
1 jar (16 ounces) large, pimiento-stuffed green olives
8 ounces spaghetti
1 jar (16 ounces) pasta sauce, heated (2 cups)
Roasted red bell pepper slice (optional)

1 Preheat oven to 400°F. Spray baking sheet with cooking spray.

2 Combine ground beef, bread crumbs, milk, egg, onion, and garlic salt in medium bowl; mix until blended. Shape mixture into 12 (2-inch) balls; place on prepared baking sheet. Press olive, pimiento end up, into each meatball to form eyeballs. Bake 15 minutes or until meatballs are browned and cooked through.

3 Meanwhile, prepare spaghetti according to package directions. Drain.

4 Toss spaghetti with pasta sauce. Top pasta with eyeballs and red pepper slice for tongue, if desired. Serve immediately.   Makes 6 to 8 servings

Birch Bark Sandwich

1 (10-inch) flour tortilla
1 tablespoon mayonnaise
1 teaspoon mustard
4 slices (about 6×4-inch) deli ham
1 teaspoon whipped cream cheese

1 Spread one side of tortilla with mayonnaise and mustard. Lay ham slices on tortilla, overlapping to cover, leaving about 2 inches uncovered at top of tortilla. Tightly roll tortilla, forming log.

2 Trim ends. Slice off about a third of log diagonally. Spread diagonal cut of smaller log with cream cheese; "glue" it to the side of a larger piece to look like a branch.

Makes 1 serving

Haunted Tip

These sandwiches can easily be scaled up to prepare enough for any number of servings. Feel free to substitute any preferred deli meat for the ham.

Chiles of Doom

1 package (8 ounces) red beans and rice mix
2 cups salsa
4 medium pasilla chiles or green bell peppers
½ cup shredded Mexican cheese blend

1 Preheat oven to 325°F. Prepare beans and rice mix according to package directions.

2 Spread salsa in shallow 12-inch baking dish. Cut chiles in half lengthwise. Remove seeds and membranes with spoon. Arrange chiles, cut sides up, on salsa. Fill chile halves with beans and rice mixture.

3 Bake 30 minutes. Remove from oven. Spoon salsa in baking dish over chiles; sprinkle with cheese. Return to oven 5 to 10 minutes or until cheese melts and mixture is bubbly.

Makes 8 servings

Haunted Tip

For the best effect, the pasilla chiles look the most misshapen and twisted.

Cowboy in a Shroud

1 pound boneless skinless chicken thighs or breasts

1 cup chicken broth

2 cans (11 ounces each) condensed nacho cheese soup, undiluted

1 can (about 14 ounces) diced tomatoes

1 can (4 ounces) diced green chiles, drained

6 (8-inch) flour tortillas

1 cup Mexican cheese blend

4 roasted red peppers

   Capers or peppercorns

   Fresh minced cilantro

1 Preheat oven to 350°F. Place chicken and broth in small saucepan. Cover; cook over low heat 20 minutes or until chicken reaches internal temperature of 180°F. Remove from heat; reserve broth. Cut chicken into bite-size strips. Set aside.

2 Combine nacho cheese soup, tomatoes, and chiles in large bowl. Divide tomato mixture in half. Add chicken to one half of tomato mixture and ½ cup reserved chicken broth to the other half.

3 Spoon chicken mixture down center of each flour tortilla; roll up. Tortillas will be very full. Pour half of nacho-chicken broth mixture into 9- to 10-inch square glass baking dish. Arrange filled tortillas seam-side down in baking dish, packing tightly. Spoon on remaining nacho-chicken broth mixture. Sprinkle with cheese.

4 Bake 20 to 25 minutes or until filling is heated through and cheese is melted. Garnish with slice of roasted red pepper, cut into 3-inch triangle for "bandana." Make cowboy face with capers and sprinkle with cilantro.

Makes 6 servings

Monster Claws

2 tablespoons flour

1 tablespoon plus 2 teaspoons cajun seasoning, divided

1 pound boneless skinless chicken breasts, cut lengthwise into ¾-inch strips

1½ cups cornflake crumbs

2 tablespoons chopped green onion

3 eggs, lightly beaten

1 red, yellow, or orange bell pepper, cut into triangles

Barbecue sauce

1 Preheat oven to 350°F. Lightly grease baking sheets. Place flour and 2 teaspoons cajun seasoning in large resealable food storage bag. Add chicken and seal. Shake bag to coat chicken.

2 Combine cornflake crumbs, green onion, and remaining 1 tablespoon cajun seasoning in large shallow bowl; mix well. Place eggs in medium shallow bowl. Dip each chicken strip into eggs and then into crumb mixture. Place coated chicken strips on prepared baking sheet.

3 Bake chicken strips 8 to 10 minutes or until chicken is no longer pink in center.

4 When chicken is cool enough to handle, make ½-inch slit in thinner end. Place bell pepper triangle into slit to form claw nail. Serve claws with barbecue sauce.

Makes about 30 strips

Trick-or-Treat Pizza Biscuits

1 can (8 biscuits) refrigerated jumbo biscuits

3 tablespoons prepared pizza sauce

Assorted pizza toppings such as cooked crumbled Italian sausage, pepperoni slices, sliced mushrooms, and/or black olives

½ cup (1 ounce) shredded mozzarella cheese or pizza cheese blend

1 egg yolk

1 teaspoon water

Assorted food colorings

1 Preheat oven to 375°F.

2 Press 4 biscuits into 4-inch rounds on ungreased baking sheet. Spread center of each biscuit with about 2 teaspoons pizza sauce. Place pizza toppings on each biscuit; top with 2 tablespoons cheese. Press remaining 4 biscuits into 4-inch rounds and place over cheese; press edges together to seal. Press design into top of each biscuit with cookie cutter, being careful not to cut all the way through top biscuit.

3 Combine egg yolk and water in small bowl. Divide yolk mixture among several small bowls; tint each with desired food coloring. Decorate imprints with egg yolk paints. Bake 12 to 15 minutes or until biscuits are golden brown at edges.

Makes 4 servings

Haunted Tip

This recipe tastes best when made with regular biscuits instead of butter-flavored biscuits.

Feet of Meat

2½ pounds ground beef

½ cup bread crumbs or oatmeal

½ cup milk or water

1 egg

1 envelope (1 ounce) dry onion soup mix

1 clove garlic, minced

8 Brazil nuts or almonds

2 tablespoons barbecue sauce or ketchup

1 Preheat oven to 350°F.

2 Combine ground beef, bread crumbs, milk, egg, soup mix, and garlic in large bowl; stir until well blended. Reserve 1 cup meat mixture.

3 Divide remaining meat mixture in half; shape each half into 7×4-inch oval. Place ovals on rimmed baking sheet. Divide reserved 1 cup meat mixture into 8 balls; place 4 balls at end of each oval for toes. Press 1 nut into each toe for toenails. Brush meat loaves with barbecue sauce.

4 Bake 1½ hours or until cooked through (160°F).   Makes 8 to 10 servings

Haunted Tip

When shaping feet, form ankles that have been "cut off" and fill with dripping ketchup before serving for an especially gruesome effect!

Jack-o'-Lantern Chili Cups

2 cans (about 11 ounces each) refrigerated corn breadstick dough
   (8 breadsticks each)

1 can (15 ounces) mild chili with beans

1 cup frozen corn

6 slices Cheddar cheese

   Olive slices, bell pepper, and carrot pieces

1 Preheat oven to 425°F. Lightly grease 16 standard (2½-inch) muffin cups.

2 Lightly roll out corn breadstick dough; press together perforations. Cut out 16 circles with 3-inch-round cookie cutter. Press 1 circle onto bottom and 1 inch up side of each prepared muffin cup.

3 Combine chili and corn in medium bowl. Fill each muffin cup with 1 tablespoon chili. Cut out 16 circles from cheese with 2-inch-round cookie cutter; place rounds over chili mixture in cups. Decorate cheese with olive, bell pepper, and carrot pieces to resemble jack-o'-lanterns.

4 Bake 10 to 12 minutes or until corn bread is completely baked and cheese is melted.   Makes about 8 servings

Lumberjack's Fingers

8 small sandwich rolls
4 hot dogs
  Ketchup
1 radish

1 Use handle of wooden spoon to push 2-inch-long hole into 1 end of each sandwich roll. Do not push spoon all the way through roll.

2 Slice each hot dog in half crosswise, then cut notch in uncut end for nail bed. Cook hot dogs according to package directions.

3 Spoon a little ketchup into hole of each roll. Push piece of hot dog into each hole, with notched end sticking out.

4 Cut 8 thin slices of radish; trim into wedges. Place radish wedge on notched end of each hot dog to make "fingernails." Serve with additional ketchup for dipping.

Makes 4 to 8 servings

Meaty Bones

½ cup hickory smoked barbecue sauce

¼ cup grape jelly

2 tablespoons steak sauce

1 teaspoon grated orange peel

12 chicken drumsticks, patted dry

Salt and black pepper

12 pieces of gauze, 12 inches each

1 Preheat broiler. Spray broiler rack and pan with nonstick cooking spray.

2 Combine barbecue sauce, jelly, steak sauce, and orange peel in small microwavable bowl. Microwave on HIGH 1 minute or until jelly is melted. Stir to blend. Divide sauce in half. Arrange chicken on prepared rack. Sprinkle lightly with salt and pepper.

3 Broil 25 to 30 minutes or until no longer pink in center, turning frequently. During the last 5 minutes of broiling, baste chicken with half of sauce. Remove from oven.

4 Dip drumsticks in reserved half of sauce. Let stand 5 minutes to cool slightly. Wrap bottom portion of each drumstick with strip of gauze.

Makes 12 drumsticks

Mini Pickle Sea Monster Burgers

4 large hamburger buns, split
2 whole dill pickles
1 pound ground beef
2 tablespoons steak sauce
Salt and black pepper
3 slices American cheese, each cut into 4 squares
Ketchup

1 Preheat broiler. Spray broiler rack and pan with nonstick cooking spray.

2 Cut 3 circles out of each bun half with 2-inch biscuit cutter. (Save scraps for another use.)

3 Cut pickles lengthwise into thin slices. Using 12 largest slices, cut 4 to 5 slits on one end of each slice, about ½ inch deep; fan slightly to resemble fish tails. (Save remaining slices for another use.)

4 Combine ground beef and steak sauce in medium bowl; mix just until blended. Shape meat into 12 (2½×¼-inch) patties. Place on prepared broiler rack. Sprinkle with salt and pepper.

5 Broil 4 inches from heat 2 minutes. Turn patties; broil 2 minutes or until no longer pink in center. Remove from heat; top with cheese squares. Arrange bun bottoms on serving platter; top with ketchup and pickle slices, making sure slices stick out of both ends. Place cheeseburgers on top of pickles; top with bun tops. Place drop of ketchup on uncut end of pickles for eyes.   Makes 12 mini burgers

Haunted Tip

To save time, look for mini buns at the supermarket instead of cutting the large hamburger buns.

Bat Wings with Drip Sauce

24 chicken wings (3 to 4 pounds)
 1 cup soy sauce
¾ cup unsulphured molasses
½ cup beef broth
½ teaspoon ground ginger
 1 cup ketchup
 2 tablespoons dark brown sugar
 2 tablespoons red wine vinegar
 1 tablespoon Dijon mustard
 1 tablespoon sesame oil
 1 teaspoon hot sauce

1 Preheat oven to 375°F.

2 Stretch out each chicken wing to resemble bat's wing. Arrange wings in single layer in large roasting pan.

3 Combine soy sauce, molasses, broth, and ginger in small saucepan; heat over low heat until mixture is smooth and well blended. Pour evenly over wings. Bake wings 30 minutes; turn and bake 30 minutes or until sauce is thickened.

4 Meanwhile, combine ketchup, brown sugar, vinegar, mustard, sesame oil, and hot sauce in small saucepan. Heat over medium heat until bubbly, stirring occasionally. Let cool slightly before serving with chicken.   Makes 8 servings

Monster Mouths

1 teaspoon vegetable oil

1 medium onion, chopped

4 slices bacon, chopped

1 pound ground beef

2 medium plum tomatoes, seeded and chopped

4 slices American cheese, chopped

½ teaspoon salt

¼ teaspoon black pepper

½ (12-ounce) package jumbo pasta shells (about 18 shells), cooked and drained
    Baby carrots, olives, red bell pepper, small pickles, and cheese slices

1 Preheat oven to 350°F. Lightly grease 13×9-inch baking dish.

2 Heat oil in large skillet over medium heat. Add onion and bacon; cook until onion is tender. Add beef; cook and stir about 5 minutes or until beef is no longer pink. Stir in tomatoes, cheese, salt, and black pepper. Spoon mixture into cooked shells; place in prepared baking dish.

3 Cut carrots into very thin strips. Cut small slit in each olive; poke one end of thin carrot strip into each olive for "eye." Cut red bell pepper into fang shapes. Slice pickle lengthwise to make tongue shape. Cut cheese slice into zigzag pattern for teeth.

4 Bake 3 to 5 minutes or until heated through; remove from oven. Decorate as desired with olive and carrot eyes, bell pepper fangs, pickle tongue, and cheese teeth. Serve immediately.   Makes about 6 servings

Pumpkin Pot Pies

6 sugar pumpkins or acorn squash (1 to 2 pounds each)
   Salt and black pepper
6 tablespoons butter
6 tablespoons all-purpose flour
3 cups chicken broth
8 ounces frozen mixed vegetables
8 ounces frozen pearl onions or chopped onions
4 cups cooked chicken, cut into bite-size pieces
1 tablespoon *each* dried thyme and dried sage
2 tablespoons finely chopped fresh parsley
1 refrigerated pie crust dough
1 egg
1 tablespoon milk

1 Preheat oven to 375°F.

2 Slice tops off pumpkins; remove seeds and pulp. Sprinkle insides of pumpkins with salt and pepper. Place cut side up on baking sheet; cover with foil.

3 Bake 25 to 30 minutes or just until skin is easily pierced with knife. Remove from oven. Reduce oven temperature to 350°F.

4 Melt butter in large saucepan over medium heat. Add flour; cook and stir 1 minute or until well blended. Add broth; cook and stir 5 minutes or until mixture is thick and bubbly. Stir in vegetables, onions, chicken, thyme, sage, and parsley. Remove from heat. Divide mixture evenly among cooled pumpkin shells.

5 Place pie crust on lightly floured work surface. Cut twelve 6-inch-long, ½-inch-wide strips with sharp paring knife. Roll dough to resemble tendrils. Cut small leaf shapes. Press lines into leaf to resemble veins with back of knife.

6 Whisk egg and milk in small bowl. Attach dough strips with egg wash, twisting gently to form coils. Attach leaves. Brush all decorations with egg wash. Return pumpkins to oven. Bake 30 minutes or until dough is golden and filling is heated through.

Makes 6 servings

Sandwich Monsters

1 package (about 16 ounces) refrigerated biscuit dough (8 biscuits)
1 cup (4 ounces) shredded mozzarella cheese
⅓ cup sliced mushrooms
2 ounces pepperoni slices (about 35 slices), quartered
½ cup pizza sauce, plus additional for dipping
1 egg, beaten

1 Preheat oven to 350°F. Line baking sheet with parchment paper or foil.

2 Separate dough into individual biscuits; set 1 biscuit aside. Roll out each of remaining biscuits on lightly floured surface to 7-inch circle. Top half of each circle evenly with cheese, mushrooms, pepperoni, and sauce, leaving ½-inch border. Fold dough over filling to form half-moon shape; seal edges with fork. Brush tops with egg.

3 Split remaining biscuit horizontally and cut each half into 8 (¼-inch) strips. For each sandwich, roll 2 strips dough into spirals to create eyes. Divide remaining 2 strips dough into 7 pieces to create noses. Arrange eyes along straight edge of each sandwich; place nose between eyes. Brush eyes and nose with egg. Place on prepared baking sheet.

4 Bake 20 to 25 minutes or until golden brown. Let stand 5 minutes before serving. Serve warm with additional pizza sauce.   Makes 7 sandwiches

Haunted Tip

Don't worry about leaking sauce or cheese—it will look like it's coming from the monster's mouth!

Slimy Sliders

1 pork tenderloin (about 1 pound)
1 cup (8 ounces) barbecue sauce
10 round dinner rolls (2½-inch diameter), sliced and warmed
½ cup prepared guacamole
20 large pimiento-stuffed olives

1 Preheat oven to 450°F. Place tenderloin in small roasting pan and brush lightly with 1 to 2 tablespoons barbecue sauce. (To avoid cross-contamination, do not dip brush into remaining sauce.)

2 Bake 30 minutes or until cooked through (160°F). Let rest 10 minutes before slicing into thin slices.

3 Spoon about 1 teaspoon barbecue sauce onto roll bottoms (warm the sauce first, if desired). Top sauce with 2 to 3 slices of tenderloin. Spoon additional 1 teaspoon sauce over top. Spoon 1 to 2 teaspoons of guacamole around edge of pork slices. Place tops on rolls.

4 Thread an olive onto each of 20 decorative picks. Push 2 picks into top of each slider to form eyes. Serve warm.   Makes 10 sliders

Haunted Tip

Substitute 1 (18-ounce) package shredded pork in barbecue sauce for the tenderloin and barbecue sauce in the recipe. Heat according to package directions.

Sticky Rice Coffins

1 cup uncooked sushi or short-grain rice

1½ cups water

3 tablespoons rice vinegar

1½ tablespoons sugar

⅛ teaspoon salt

1 tablespoon vegetable oil

1 small red onion, finely chopped

1 clove garlic, minced

1 bag (8 ounces) cooked peeled baby shrimp, thawed and drained

1 tablespoon minced fresh cilantro

1 cup coconut milk

1 tablespoon curry powder or Thai green curry paste

1 Combine rice and water in medium saucepan. Bring to a boil. Reduce heat to low; cover and cook 15 minutes or until liquid is absorbed. Set aside.

2 Combine vinegar, sugar, and salt in small microwavable bowl. Microwave on HIGH 30 seconds or until sugar dissolves. Slowly pour vinegar mixture over rice, stirring until liquid is absorbed and rice is sticky. (It may not be necessary to add all the vinegar mixture.) Set aside to cool.

3 Heat oil in medium skillet. Add onion and garlic; cook and stir 2 minutes. Add shrimp; cook 2 minutes. Stir shrimp mixture and cilantro into rice.

4 Scoop rice mixture into ⅓-cup measuring cup or small mold. Pack down. Turn out onto serving plate. Press rice into coffin shape, using wet spatula. Combine coconut milk and curry powder in small bowl. Drizzle over rice or serve as dipping sauce. Makes 10 servings

Snake Calzone

2 loaves (16 ounces each) frozen white bread dough, thawed

4 tablespoons mustard, divided

2 tablespoons sun-dried tomato pesto, divided

2 teaspoons Italian seasoning, divided

10 ounces thinly sliced ham, divided

10 ounces thinly sliced salami, divided

1½ cups (6 ounces) shredded provolone cheese, divided

1½ cups (6 ounces) shredded mozzarella cheese, divided

2 egg yolks, divided

2 teaspoons water, divided

Red and yellow liquid food colorings

Olive slices and bell pepper strips

1 Line 2 baking sheets with parchment paper; spray with nonstick cooking spray. Roll out 1 loaf of dough into 24×6-inch rectangle on lightly floured surface. Spread 2 tablespoons mustard and 1 tablespoon pesto over dough, leaving 1-inch border; sprinkle with 1 teaspoon Italian seasoning.

2 Layer half of ham and salami over dough. Sprinkle ¾ cup of each cheese over meats. Brush edges of dough with water. Beginning at long side, tightly roll up dough. Pinch edges to seal. Transfer roll to prepared baking sheet, seam side down; shape into S-shaped snake or coiled snake (leave one end unattached to form head on coil). Repeat with remaining bread dough and ingredients.

3 Combine 1 egg yolk, 1 teaspoon water, and red food coloring in small bowl. Combine remaining egg yolk, remaining 1 teaspoon water, and yellow food coloring in separate small bowl. Paint stripes, dots, and zigzags over dough with pastry brush to create snakeskin pattern.

4 Let dough rise, uncovered, in warm place 30 minutes. (Let dough rise 40 minutes if using a coil shape.) Preheat oven to 375°F. Taper one end of each roll to form head and one end to form tail. Score tail end to form rattlers, if desired.

5 Bake 25 to 30 minutes. Cool slightly. Attach olives for eyes and bell pepper strips for tongues with small amount of mustard. Slice and serve warm.

Makes 24 to 28 servings

Slimy Snails

8 ounces mostaccioli or penne rigate pasta

½ package (8 ounces) gnocchi pasta shells*

2 packages (1½ ounces each) four-cheese sauce mix for pasta, prepared according to package directions

1 can (4¼ ounces) chopped black olives

½ cup chopped fresh parsley

1 tablespoon paprika

¼ cup shredded carrots

*Pasta shells can be used in place of gnocchi. Cooked lasagna noodles can be rolled or coiled to form a snail as another option.

1 Prepare pasta and cheese sauce according to package directions. Reserve 8 mostaccioli and gnocchi noodles and ¼ cup cheese sauce to make snails.

2 Layer remaining mostaccioli and gnocchi with warm cheese sauce in 13×9-inch pan or serving dish. Sprinkle with black olives and parsley. Keep warm while assembling snails.

3 Sprinkle reserved shells with paprika. Assemble snails by placing 1 shell on top of each mostaccioli noodle, using small amount of sauce inside shell to adhere. Insert 2 small shredded carrots at top of each snail for antennae. Place on top of prepared dish. Serve warm. Makes 8 servings

Backbones

4 (10-inch) flour tortillas

1 package (3½ ounces) soft cheese spread with herbs

1 bag (6 ounces) fresh baby spinach

½ pound thinly sliced salami or ham

½ pound thinly sliced Havarti or Swiss cheese

1 jar (7 ounces) roasted red bell peppers, drained and sliced into thin strips

1 Spread each tortilla with 2 to 3 tablespoons cheese spread. Layer each tortilla evenly with one fourth of spinach, salami, cheese, and red bell pepper strips; roll up. (Slice off and discard rounded ends, if desired.) Repeat with remaining ingredients.

2 Cut tortilla rolls into 1½-inch slices; secure with toothpicks. To serve, stack slices in threes on serving plate. Makes 18 servings

Haunted Taco Tarts

1 tablespoon vegetable oil
½ cup chopped onion
½ pound ground turkey
1 clove garlic, minced
½ teaspoon dried oregano
½ teaspoon chili powder
¼ teaspoon salt
    Egg Yolk Paint (recipe follows)
1 package (15 ounces) refrigerated pie crust dough
1 egg white
½ cup chopped tomato
½ cup taco-flavored shredded cheese

1 Heat oil in large skillet over medium heat. Add onion; cook until tender. Add turkey; cook until turkey is no longer pink, stirring occasionally. Stir in garlic, oregano, chili powder, and salt; set aside.

2 Preheat oven to 375°F. Lightly grease baking sheets. Prepare Egg Yolk Paint; set aside.

3 Roll 1 pie crust to 14-inch diameter on lightly floured surface. Cut out pairs of desired shapes using 3-inch Halloween cookie cutters. Repeat with second pie crust, rerolling dough if necessary. Place ½ of shapes on prepared baking sheets. Brush edges with egg white. Spoon about 1 tablespoon taco mixture onto each shape. Sprinkle with 1 teaspoon tomato and 1 teaspoon cheese. Top with remaining matching shapes; press edges to seal. Decorate with Egg Yolk Paint.

4 Bake 10 to 12 minutes or until golden brown.   Makes 14 tarts

Egg Yolk Paint
    4 egg yolks, divided
    4 teaspoons water, divided
        Red, yellow, blue, and green liquid food colorings

Place 1 egg yolk in each of 4 small bowls. Add 1 teaspoon water and a few drops different food coloring to each; beat lightly.

Mummy Dogs

1 can (11 ounces) refrigerated breadstick dough (8 breadsticks)
1 package (16 ounces) hot dogs
  Mustard
  Poppy seeds

1 Preheat oven to 375°F.

2 Using 1 dough strip for each, wrap hot dogs to look like mummies, leaving opening for eyes. Place on ungreased baking sheet.

3 Bake 12 to 15 minutes or until light golden brown. Place dots of mustard and poppy seeds for eyes.   Makes 8 servings

Mini Mummy Dogs

Use 1 package (16 ounces) mini hot dogs instead of regular hot dogs. Cut each breadstick strip into 3 pieces. Cut each piece in half lengthwise. Using 1 strip of dough for each, wrap and bake mini hot dogs as directed above.

Toasted Cheese Jack-o'-Lanterns

3 tablespoons butter or margarine, softened
8 slices bread
4 slices Monterey Jack cheese
4 slices sharp Cheddar cheese

 1 Preheat oven to 350°F. Spread butter on one side of each bread slice. Place bread, buttered side down, onto ungreased cookie sheet.

2 Cut out shapes from 4 bread slices using paring knife to make jack-o'-lantern faces. Layer 1 slice Monterey Jack and 1 slice Cheddar on remaining 4 bread slices.

3 Bake 10 to 12 minutes or until cheese is melted. Remove from oven; place jack-o'-lantern bread slice on sandwiches. Serve immediately.

Makes 4 servings

Witch's Cauldron Pasta with Breadstick Brooms

1 pound uncooked rotini or cavatappi pasta
1 package (10 ounces) frozen chopped spinach, thawed and squeezed dry
1 package (3 ounces) cream cheese
½ teaspoon ground nutmeg
1 jar (16 ounces) alfredo pasta sauce
   Breadstick Brooms (recipe follows)

1 Cook pasta according to package directions; drain.

2 Meanwhile, combine spinach, cream cheese, and nutmeg in blender or food processor; blend until smooth. Combine spinach mixture and alfredo sauce in medium saucepan over low heat; cook and stir until heated through.

3 Toss hot cooked pasta with sauce in large serving bowl until evenly coated. Serve with Breadstick Brooms.   Makes 4 to 6 servings

Breadstick Brooms

1 package (11 ounces) refrigerated breadstick dough

1 Preheat oven to 375°F.

2 Unroll dough and divide along perforations. For each broom, shape breadstick into 8×1½-inch strip; twist one end for handle. Cut 5 or 6 slits (2 inches long) into opposite end; separate dough at slits. Place about 2 inches apart on ungreased baking sheets.

3 Bake 15 to 18 minutes or until golden brown.   Makes 12 breadsticks

Devilish Delights

1 package (16 ounces) hot roll mix plus ingredients to prepare mix
2 tablespoons vegetable oil, divided
1 pound boneless skinless chicken breasts, cut into ¾-inch pieces
¾ cup chopped onion
1 clove garlic, minced
1¼ cups sliced zucchini
1 can (about 8 ounces) peeled diced tomatoes, drained
1 can (4 ounces) sliced mushrooms, drained
1 teaspoon dried basil
½ teaspoon dried oregano
Salt and black pepper
1 cup (4 ounces) shredded mozzarella cheese
1 egg yolk
1 teaspoon water
Red food coloring

1 Prepare hot roll mix according to package directions. Knead dough about 5 minutes on floured surface until smooth. Cover loosely; let stand 15 minutes.

2 Heat 1 tablespoon oil in large skillet over medium-high heat. Add chicken; cook 5 to 6 minutes or until cooked through. Remove from skillet; set aside. Cook and stir onion and garlic in remaining 1 tablespoon oil in skillet until tender. Stir in zucchini, tomatoes, mushrooms, basil, and oregano; bring to a boil. Reduce heat. Simmer 5 to 10 minutes or until liquid has evaporated. Stir in chicken; cook 1 minute. Remove from heat. Season with salt and pepper. Stir in cheese.

3 Preheat oven to 400°F. Grease baking sheets.

4 Roll dough on floured surface to ¼-inch thickness. Cut into 20 (4-inch) circles. Place 10 circles on prepared baking sheets; spoon chicken mixture evenly on circles. Top with remaining circles; seal edges. Cut vents for devil and use dough scraps to make horns, eyes, nose, and beard. Combine egg yolk and water; brush dough. Add red food coloring to remaining egg yolk mixture; brush horns and beard.

5 Bake 20 to 25 minutes or until golden.

Makes 10 servings

Sips 'n' Sweets

Black Cat Cupcakes

1 package (about 18 ounces) cake mix, any flavor,
 plus ingredients to prepare mix
1 container (16 ounces) chocolate fudge frosting
 White decorating icing
 Graham crackers
 Black string licorice
 Assorted candies

1 Preheat oven to 350°F. Line 24 standard (2½-inch) muffin cups with paper baking cups.

2 Prepare cake mix according to package directions. Spoon batter into prepared muffin cups, filling two-thirds full.

3 Bake 20 minutes or until toothpick inserted into centers comes out clean. Cool in pans 10 minutes. Remove to wire racks; cool completely.

4 Frost cupcakes. Pipe two mounds in center of each cupcake for cheeks. Pipe mouths using white decorating icing. Cut graham crackers into small triangles; press into cupcakes for ears. Decorate cat faces with licorice and assorted candies.

Makes 24 cupcakes

Autumn Leaves

1½ cups (3 sticks) unsalted butter, softened

¾ cup packed light brown sugar

½ teaspoon vanilla

3½ cups all-purpose flour

1 teaspoon ground cinnamon

½ teaspoon salt

⅛ teaspoon ground ginger

⅛ teaspoon ground cloves

2 tablespoons unsweetened cocoa powder

Yellow, orange, and red food coloring

⅓ cup semisweet chocolate chips

1 Beat butter, brown sugar, and vanilla in large bowl with electric mixer at medium speed until light and fluffy. Add flour, cinnamon, salt, ginger, and cloves; beat at low speed until well blended.

2 Divide dough into 5 equal sections. Stir cocoa into 1 section until well blended. (If dough is too dry and will not hold together, add 1 teaspoon water; beat until well blended and dough forms a ball.) Stir yellow food coloring into 1 section until well blended and desired shade is reached. Repeat with 2 sections and orange and red food colorings. Leave remaining 1 section plain.

3 Preheat oven to 350°F. Lightly grease cookie sheets. Working with half of each dough color, press colors together lightly. Roll dough on lightly floured surface to ¼-inch thickness. Cut dough with leaf-shaped cookie cutters of various shapes and sizes. Place similarly sized cutouts 2 inches apart on prepared cookie sheets. Repeat with remaining dough and scraps.

4 Bake 10 to 15 minutes or until edges are lightly browned. Remove to wire racks; cool completely.

5 Place chocolate chips in small resealable food storage bag; seal. Microwave on HIGH 1 minute; knead bag lightly. Microwave on HIGH at additional 30-second intervals until chips are completely melted, kneading bag after each interval. Cut off tiny corner of bag. Pipe chocolate onto cookies in vein patterns.

Makes about 2 dozen cookies

Bloody Blast

3 cans (12 ounces each) tomato or vegetable juice
2 tablespoons Worcestershire sauce
1 tablespoon prepared horseradish
1 tablespoon lemon juice
¼ to ½ teaspoon hot pepper sauce
    Celery stalks and pimiento-stuffed olives (optional)

1 Combine tomato juice, Worcestershire sauce, horseradish, lemon juice, and hot pepper sauce in punch bowl. Chill at least 1 hour.

2 Pour into ice-filled glasses. Garnish with celery stalks and olives for eyes.

Makes 6 servings

Bobbing Head Punch

    Assorted candies
    Assorted fruit slices and pieces
    Water
6 cups white grape juice
4 cups ginger ale
2 cups apple juice or 2 additional cups ginger ale
    Green food coloring

1 Arrange candy and fruit slices in bottom of 9-inch glass pie plate to create a face. (Remember, the bottom of face is what will show in the punch bowl.) Add water to cover face; carefully place in freezer. Freeze overnight.

2 At time of serving, add juice and ginger ale to 4- to 5-quart punch bowl. Tint mixture green. Invert pie plate, placing one hand underneath, run under cold running water to release frozen face. Place ice mold upside down on top of juice mixture; serve.

Makes 20 cups

Bloody Blast

Creamy Dreamy Taco Tomb Treats

¼ cup plus 2 tablespoons packed light brown sugar

2 egg whites

2 tablespoons butter, melted and slightly cooled

1 teaspoon vanilla

½ teaspoon ground cinnamon

¼ teaspoon ground nutmeg

½ cup pecans or walnuts, chopped

2 tablespoons all-purpose flour

2 cups vanilla or chocolate ice cream

Fresh chopped strawberries and pineapple

Chocolate sprinkles

1 Preheat oven to 375°F.

2 Beat brown sugar, egg whites, butter, vanilla, cinnamon, and nutmeg in medium bowl with electric mixer at medium speed 1 minute. Combine pecans and flour in food processor or blender; pulse until coarsely ground. Add to sugar mixture; stir until well blended. Let stand 10 minutes to thicken.

3 Spray baking sheet with nonstick cooking spray. Spoon 2 tablespoons batter onto sheet. Spread into 5-inch circle using back of spoon. Repeat with another 2 tablespoons batter, placed 4 to 5 inches apart.

4 Bake 5 minutes or until light brown. Cool on wire rack 1 minute. Gently remove each cookie with metal spatula and place over rolling pin. Let cool 5 minutes. Repeat with remaining batter.

5 Fill each cookie with ⅓ cup ice cream. Wrap in plastic wrap; freeze until ready to serve. Top with strawberries, pineapple, and chocolate sprinkles before serving.

Makes 6 treats

Trick-or-Treat Caramel Apples

5 medium apples

1 package (14 ounces) chocolate caramels

1 cup miniature marshmallows

1 tablespoon water

Candy corn, red cinnamon candies, jelly beans, licorice whips, colored sprinkles, and other assorted candies for decoration

1 Place 5 (2½-inch) paper baking cups on baking sheet. Flatten cups. Rinse and thoroughly dry apples. Insert wooden sticks into stem ends.

2 Combine caramels, marshmallows, and water in medium saucepan. Cook over medium heat, stirring constantly, until caramels melt. Remove from heat.

3 Dip apple into caramel mixture, coating thoroughly. Remove excess caramel mixture by scraping apple bottom across rim of saucepan. Place in cup on prepared baking sheet. Immediately decorate with candies to create face or other design. Repeat with remaining apples. Refrigerate until firm.   Makes 5 servings

Popcorn Ghosts

1 package (10 ounces) regular marshmallows
¼ cup (½ stick) butter
6 cups popcorn or puffed rice cereal
1 pound white candy coating or white chocolate, melted
24 mini chocolate chips
    Black string licorice, cut into 2-inch lengths

1 Combine marshmallows and butter in large saucepan. Cook and stir over medium heat until mixture is melted and smooth. Stir in popcorn; mix well.

2 Form each ghost with about 1 cup popcorn mixture. Let ghosts cool completely on wire rack set over waxed paper.

3 Spoon melted candy coating over each ghost to cover completely. Use fork to create folds and drapes in coating. Decorate with mini chocolate chips for eyes and licorice for mouths.

Makes about 12 ghosts

Boo! Brew

4 cups cranberry-raspberry juice

2 cups white grape juice

8 whole cloves

1 small orange, sliced (with peel)

1 medium lemon, sliced (with peel)

   Multicolored candy sticks or peppermint sticks (optional)

1 Bring juices, cloves, orange, and lemon just to a boil in large saucepan. Reduce heat and simmer, uncovered, 15 minutes.

2 Strain into pitcher or bowl, removing and discarding cloves and fruit. Pour into cups; add candy sticks, if desired.   *Makes 5 cups*

Haunted Tip

Brew can be kept warm and served from a slow cooker. For more citrus flavor, remove mixture from heat and let stand 30 minutes, or make ahead and refrigerate until needed, reheating at serving time.

Spider Cakes

18 chocolate cupcakes

1 box (4-serving size) white chocolate pudding and pie filling mix, prepared according to package directions and tinted green with food coloring

1 container (16 ounces) fudge frosting

72 pieces black licorice, cut in half

36 red cinnamon candies

2 black licorice strings, cut into ¼-inch pieces (optional)

Fruit leather

1 Place 18 (2½-inch) paper baking cups on baking sheet. Flatten cups.

2 Poke small hole in the bottom of each cupcake with toothpick. Cut tiny corner off of large food storage bag, making just large enough for small, round piping tip to fit through. Place tip through bag and into hole.

3 Spoon green pudding into bag. Insert piping tip into bottom of cupcake. Pipe some pudding gently and slowly into cupcake. Repeat with remaining cupcakes.

4 Frost tops and sides of cupcakes. Place each cupcake, unfrosted side down, on prepared baking sheet.

5 Insert 4 licorice pieces into each side of cupcake to form legs. Press in cinnamon candies for eyes. Press licorice strings around cinnamon candies to create eyelashes, if desired. Cut mouths from fruit leather and press to face. Serve immediately. Makes 18 cupcakes

Note: Spiders will ooze green "blood" when bitten or sliced.

Friendly Ghost Cupcakes

1⅓ cups all-purpose flour

¾ cup unsweetened cocoa powder

2 teaspoons baking powder

½ teaspoon salt

¼ teaspoon baking soda

1 cup sugar

6 tablespoons (¾ stick) unsalted butter, softened

2 eggs

1 teaspoon vanilla

¾ cup milk

1 cup prepared chocolate frosting

4 cups whipped topping

Mini semisweet chocolate chips

1 Preheat oven to 350°F. Line 14 standard (2½-inch) muffin cups with paper baking cups.

2 Whisk flour, cocoa powder, baking powder, salt, and baking soda in medium bowl. Beat sugar and butter in large bowl with electric mixer at medium speed until fluffy. Add eggs and vanilla; beat until well blended. Add flour mixture and milk; beat at low speed just until combined. Spoon batter evenly into prepared muffin cups.

3 Bake 15 minutes or until toothpick inserted into centers comes out clean. Cool in pans 10 minutes. Remove to wire racks; cool completely.

4 Place frosting in medium microwavable bowl. Microwave on HIGH 10 seconds; stir. Microwave 10 seconds or just until melted. Hold cupcake upside down and dip top into melted frosting, working with one at a time. Tilt cupcake to let excess frosting drip off; return to wire rack. Let stand until set.

5 Place whipped topping in pastry bag or large resealable food storage bag with 1 inch cut off one corner of bag. Pipe ghost shape onto each cupcake (or drop whipped topping by spoonfuls onto cupcakes to resemble ghosts); add chocolate chips for eyes. Refrigerate until ready to serve.   Makes 14 cupcakes

Creepy Crawly Anthill Cake

30 chocolate sandwich cookies with vanilla cream centers

1 package (13 ounces) peppermint patties

2 quarts vanilla ice cream

20 vanilla wafers

8 to 10 chocolate-covered almonds

8 to 10 round milk chocolate-covered caramel candies

1 tube (0.6 ounce) black gel icing

Candy corn (optional)

1 For base, place chocolate sandwich cookies in food processor or blender; process to coarse crumbs. Add peppermint patties; process to coarse crumbs. Coat 10-inch springform pan with cooking spray. Add cookie mixture; press down gently to cover bottom and up ½ inch on side. Add ice cream by spoonfuls. Use back of spoon to smooth ice cream evenly on top. Cover with foil; freeze 8 hours or overnight.

2 For anthill, place vanilla wafers in food processor or blender; process until smooth. Place in large resealable food storage bag; seal. Store at room temperature until assembling cake.

3 To assemble cake, remove side of springform pan. Place cake on serving platter. Pour vanilla wafer crumbs in mound on one side of cake. Arrange "ants" on cake using one chocolate-covered almond for each body and one chocolate-covered caramel for each head. Pipe eyes and legs with icing. Garnish with candy corn.

Makes 16 servings

Voodoo Juice

1 cup distilled water, divided
12 whole strawberries
24 fresh or frozen blueberries
12 mandarin orange sections
8 cups chilled fruit punch, apple cider, or favorite soft drink

 1 Place 1 tablespoon water in each of 12 mini (1¾-inch) muffin cups of pan. Freeze 1 hour or until frozen solid.

2 Slice ¼ inch off pointed end of each strawberry. Arrange 2 blueberries at top of each cup of ice for eyes, 1 strawberry tip pointed up in center for nose, and 1 orange section directly under strawberry tip for smile. Spoon teaspoon of remaining water over each; freeze 2 hours or until frozen solid.*

3 At serving time, remove ice by placing back of muffin pan in larger pan of water until faces release.

4 Pour chilled punch into small glasses. Place 1 frozen face in each glass.

Makes 12 servings

*Frozen faces may be made up to 48 hours in advance.

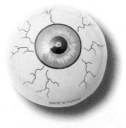

Black Cat Cookies

1 package (18 ounces) refrigerated sugar cookie dough
All-purpose flour (optional)
White Decorator Icing (recipe follows)
Black paste food coloring, divided
Red paste food coloring (optional)
Round colored candies
String licorice

1 Preheat oven to 350°F. Remove dough from wrapper according to package directions. Divide dough in half. Reserve half; cover and refrigerate remaining half.

2 Roll reserved dough on lightly floured surface to ⅛-inch thickness. Sprinkle with flour to minimize sticking, if necessary. Cut out dough using 3½-inch cat face cookie cutter. Place cutouts 2 inches apart on ungreased baking sheets. Repeat with remaining dough and scraps.

3 Bake 8 to 10 minutes or until firm but not browned. Cool on baking sheets 2 minutes. Remove to wire racks; cool completely.

4 Meanwhile, prepare White Decorator Icing. Add black food coloring, a few drops at a time, until desired shade is reached. Spread cookies with icing. Use white icing and red food coloring to highlight cats' faces, if desired. Use round candies for eyes and licorice for whiskers. Use remaining black food coloring to make eye centers. *Makes about 20 cookies*

White Decorator Icing

4 cups powdered sugar
½ cup (1 stick) unsalted butter or shortening, softened
1 tablespoon corn syrup
6 to 8 tablespoons milk

1 Beat powdered sugar, butter, corn syrup, and milk in medium bowl with electric mixer on medium speed 2 minutes or until fluffy.

Makes about 4 cups

Bloodshot Eyeballs

2¾ cups all-purpose flour

1 teaspoon baking soda

½ teaspoon salt

1 cup (2 sticks) butter, softened

¾ cup granulated sugar

¾ cup packed light brown sugar

2 eggs

1 teaspoon vanilla

1 container (16 ounces) white frosting

Green or blue gummy candy rings

1 tube (0.6 ounce) black decorating gel

1 tube (0.6 ounce) red decorating gel

1 Combine flour, baking soda, and salt in small bowl. Beat butter, granulated sugar, and brown sugar in large bowl with electric mixer on medium speed until light and fluffy. Beat in eggs, one at a time. Beat in vanilla. Add flour mixture gradually until well blended. Divide dough into 2 discs. Wrap tightly in plastic wrap; chill at least 30 minutes.

2 Preheat oven to 375°F. Roll out dough on lightly floured surface to ⅛-inch thickness. Draw oval eye shape (about 4×2 inches) on piece of cardboard. Cut out shape and use as stencil for cutting cookie dough. Place cutouts 2 inches apart on ungreased cookie sheets.

3 Bake 9 to 11 minutes or until golden brown. Remove cookies to wire racks to cool completely.

4 Spread frosting evenly over cooled cookies. Arrange candy rings in center of each eye to create iris. Fill in pupils and pipe eyelashes with black decorating gel. Decorate with red decorating gel for bloodshot effect.

Makes about 2½ dozen cookies

Blue Goo Cupcakes

1 package (about 18 ounces) white cake mix,
 plus ingredients to prepare mix

Blue food coloring

1 package (6 ounces) blue gelatin

Blue decorating icing

1 Preheat oven to 350°F. Line 24 standard (2½-inch) muffin cups with paper baking cups. Prepare cake mix according to package directions, adding food coloring, a few drops at a time, until desired shade of blue is reached. Spoon batter into prepared muffin cups, filling two-thirds full.

2 Bake 20 minutes or until toothpick inserted into centers comes out clean. Cool in pans 10 minutes. Remove to wire racks; cool completely.

3 Meanwhile, combine gelatin and 1⅓ cups boiling water in small bowl. Stir mixture 3 minutes or until gelatin is completely dissolved. Freeze mixture 40 minutes until partially set, stirring often.

4 Pipe ring of blue icing around edge of each cupcake. Spoon 1 rounded tablespoon gelatin mixture onto each cupcake. Serve immediately or refrigerate until ready to serve.   Makes 24 cupcakes

Haunted Tip

For a firm texture, or in extreme heat, chill until serving time. For a runny "blob" consistency, serve at room temperature.

Boo the Ghost

1 (13×9-inch) cake, completely cooled
2 cups Light & Fluffy Frosting (recipe follows)
2 black licorice drops or jelly beans

1 If cake top is rounded, trim horizontally with long serrated knife. Trim sides of cake. Prepare 13×9-inch cake board.

2 Draw ghost outline on 13×9-inch piece of waxed paper using photo as guide. Cut out pattern; place on cake. Cut out ghost; place on prepared cake board.

3 Prepare Light & Fluffy Frosting. Swirl frosting over ghost. Arrange licorice drops for eyes and spiders, if desired, as shown in photo.

Makes 12 to 14 servings

Light & Fluffy Frosting

⅔ cup sugar
2 egg whites
¼ cup plus 1 tablespoon light corn syrup
Dash salt
1 teaspoon vanilla

1 Combine sugar, egg whites, corn syrup, and salt in top of double boiler; set over boiling water. Beat constantly about 7 minutes or until stiff peaks form. Remove from water; beat in vanilla.

Makes about 2 cups

Trick-or-Treat Punch

7 cups water, divided
   Green food coloring (optional)
1 can (12 ounces) frozen lemonade concentrate, thawed
1 envelope (4 ounces) orange-flavored drink mix
1 bottle (2 liters) ginger ale*
   Cherry halves
   Lime slices

*For an adult party, substitute 2 bottles (750 ml each) champagne for ginger ale, if desired.

1 Line baking sheet with paper towels. Fill pitcher with 3 cups water; tint with green food coloring, if desired. Pour into food-safe glove; tightly close wrist of glove with twist tie. Place glove on prepared baking sheet. Use inverted custard cup to elevate tied end of glove to prevent leaking. Freeze overnight.

2 To serve, combine lemonade concentrate, drink mix, and remaining 4 cups water in punch bowl; stir until drink mix is dissolved and mixture is well blended. Stir in ginger ale. Cut glove away from ice; float frozen hand in punch. Insert cherry halves in centers of lime slices; float in punch.

Makes 16 (6-ounce) servings and 1 ice hand

Candy Corn Cookies

Butter Cookie Dough (recipe follows)
Cookie Glaze (recipe follows)
Yellow and orange food colorings

1 Prepare Butter Cookie Dough. Preheat oven to 350°F.

2 Roll dough on floured surface to ¼-inch thickness. Cut out 3-inch candy corn shapes from dough. Place cutouts on ungreased cookie sheets.

3 Bake 8 to 10 minutes or until edges are lightly browned. Remove to wire racks to cool completely. Prepare Cookie Glaze.

4 Place racks over waxed paper-lined baking sheets. Divide Cookie Glaze into thirds; place in separate small bowls. Tint one-third glaze with yellow food coloring and one-third with orange food coloring. Leave remaining glaze white. Spoon glazes over cookies to resemble candy corn as shown in photo. Let stand until glaze is set.   *Makes about 2 dozen cookies*

Butter Cookie Dough

1¾ cups all-purpose flour
¾ cup (1½ sticks) butter, softened
¼ cup granulated sugar
¼ cup packed light brown sugar
1 egg yolk
¾ teaspoon baking powder
⅛ teaspoon salt

1 Combine flour, butter, granulated sugar, brown sugar, egg yolk, baking powder, and salt in medium bowl; mix well. Cover; refrigerate 4 hours or until firm.

Cookie Glaze

1 Combine 4 cups powdered sugar and 4 tablespoons milk in medium bowl. Add 1 to 2 tablespoons more milk as needed to make medium-thick, pourable, glaze.   *Makes about 4 cups*

Creepy Cookie Cauldrons

1 package (18 ounces) refrigerated chocolate cookie dough*
    All-purpose flour (optional)
1 package (14 ounces) caramels
2 tablespoons milk
1 cup crisp rice cereal
¼ cup mini chocolate chips
    Black licorice whips

*If refrigerated chocolate cookie dough is unavailable, add ¼ cup unsweetened cocoa powder to refrigerated sugar cookie dough. Beat in large bowl with electric mixer on medium speed until well blended.

1 Grease 36 mini (1¾-inch) muffin cups. Remove dough from wrapper according to package directions. Sprinkle dough with flour to minimize sticking, if necessary.

2 Cut dough into 36 equal pieces; roll into balls. Place 1 ball in bottom of each muffin cup. Press dough on bottoms and up sides of muffin cups; chill 15 minutes. Preheat oven to 350°F.

3 Bake 8 to 9 minutes. (Cookies will be puffy.) Remove from oven; gently press down center of each cookie. Return to oven 1 minute. Cool cookies in muffin cups 5 minutes. Remove to wire racks; cool completely.

4 Melt caramels and milk in small saucepan over low heat until smooth, stirring frequently. Stir in cereal. Spoon 1 heaping teaspoon caramel mixture into each cookie cup. Immediately sprinkle with chocolate chips.

5 Cut licorice whips into 4½-inch lengths. For each cookie, make small slit in side; insert end of licorice strip. Repeat on other side of cookie to make cauldron handle.   Makes 3 dozen cookies

Hot Cocoa with Floating Eyeballs

16 large marshmallows

16 black licorice candies

2 quarts milk

1 cup chocolate-flavored drink mix

1 cup mint-flavored semisweet chocolate chips

1 Make slit in center of each marshmallow; insert licorice candy into slit.

2 Combine milk and drink mix in medium saucepan; stir in chocolate chips. Cook over medium heat until chips are melted and milk is heated through, stirring occasionally.

3 Fill each mug with hot cocoa and top with 2 eyeballs. Serve immediately.

Makes 8 servings

Crusty Crawlers

1 cup semisweet chocolate chips

1 cup peanut butter chips

3 cups crispy chow mein noodles

¾ cup toffee bits

18 maraschino cherries, quartered and well drained

1 Heat chocolate chips and peanut butter chips in large saucepan over low heat; stir until melted. Remove saucepan from heat; add noodles. Stir gently with rubber spatula until completely coated.

2 Spoon mixture into mounds on waxed paper. Sprinkle with toffee bits, pressing gently to adhere. Place two cherry pieces on each mound for eyes. Cool completely before serving. Makes 36 crawlers

Ghost on a Stick

4 medium pears, stems removed
9 squares (2 ounces each) almond bark
Mini chocolate chips

1 Line baking sheet with waxed paper and 4 paper baking cups. Insert wooden craft sticks into stem ends of pears.

2 Melt almond bark according to package directions. Dip pears into melted almond bark, spooning bark over tops to coat evenly. Remove excess by scraping pear bottoms across rim of measuring cup. Place on paper baking cups; let set 1 minute.

3 Decorate with mini chocolate chips to make ghost faces. Place spoonful of extra almond bark at bottom of pears for ghost tails. Refrigerate until firm.

Makes 4 servings

Magic Potion

Creepy Crawler Ice Ring (recipe follows)
1 cup boiling water
2 packages (4-serving size each) lime-flavored gelatin
3 cups cold water
1½ liters (48 ounces) lemon-lime soda, chilled
½ cup superfine sugar
Gummy worms (optional)

1 Prepare Creepy Crawler Ice Ring.

2 Pour boiling water over gelatin in heatproof punch bowl; stir until gelatin dissolves. Stir in cold water. Add lemon-lime soda and sugar; stir well (mixture will foam several minutes).

3 Before serving, unmold ice ring by dipping bottom of mold briefly into hot water; add to punch bowl. Garnish cups with gummy worms.

Makes about 10 servings

Creepy Crawler Ice Ring

1 cup gummy worms or other creepy crawler candy
1 quart lemon-lime thirst quencher beverage

1 Arrange gummy worms in bottom of 5-cup ring mold or bowl; fill mold with thirst quencher beverage. Freeze 8 hours or overnight. *Makes 1 ice ring*

Haunted Tip

This Magic Potion can easily go from creepy to cute. For the punch, use orange-flavored gelatin instead of lime. For the ice ring, use candy corn and candy pumpkins instead of gummy worms.

Peanut Butter Aliens

1 package (about 16 ounces) refrigerated sugar cookie dough
½ cup creamy peanut butter
⅓ cup all-purpose flour
¼ cup powdered sugar
½ teaspoon vanilla
   Green decorating icing
1 cup strawberry jam

1 Preheat oven to 350°F. Grease cookie sheets. Let dough stand at room temperature 15 minutes.

2 Combine dough, peanut butter, flour, powdered sugar, and vanilla in large bowl; beat with electric mixer at medium speed until well blended. Reserve half of dough; wrap and refrigerate.

3 Roll out remaining dough between parchment paper to ¼-inch thickness. Cut out 14 circles with 3-inch round cookie cutter; pinch 1 side of each circle to make teardrop shape. Place 2 inches apart on prepared cookie sheets.

4 Bake 12 to 14 minutes or until set. Cool on cookie sheets 2 minutes. Remove to wire racks; cool completely.

5 Roll out reserved dough between parchment paper to ¼-inch thickness. Cut out 14 circles with 3-inch round cookie cutter; pinch 1 side of each circle to form teardrop shape. Place 2 inches apart on prepared cookie sheets. Cut out 2 oblong holes for eyes. Make small slit for mouth. Bake 12 to 14 minutes or until set. Cool on cookie sheets 2 minutes. Remove to wire racks; cool completely.

6 Spread icing on cookies with faces. Let stand 10 minutes or until set. Spread jam on uncut cookies. Top each jam-topped cookie with green face cookie.

                                          Makes 14 sandwich cookies

Skull and Crossbones

1 package (about 21 ounces) brownie mix,
    plus ingredients to prepare mix
2 egg whites
¼ teaspoon almond extract (optional)
½ cup sugar
    Red and black decorating gel
1 container (16 ounces) chocolate frosting

1 Prepare brownies in 13×9-inch baking pan according to package directions. Cool completely in pan on wire rack.

2 Preheat oven to 250°F. Line baking sheet with parchment paper.

3 Beat egg whites in large bowl with electric mixer on medium speed until foamy. Add almond extract, if desired; beat until soft peaks form. Gradually add sugar; beat until stiff peaks form. Fill pastry bag with egg white mixture. Pipe 24 skull and cross bone shapes onto prepared baking sheet.

4 Bake 12 minutes or until very lightly browned and set. Cool completely on pan on wire rack. Carefully remove meringues from parchment paper. Decorate with red gel for eyes and black gel for mouths.

5 Frost brownies; cut into 24 rectangles. Place one meringue on each brownie.
Makes 2 dozen brownies

Spooky French Silk Cream Tarts

½ cup sugar

½ cup unsweetened cocoa

⅓ cup all-purpose flour

¼ teaspoon salt

1¾ cups whole milk

⅔ cup semisweet chocolate chips

1 cup whipped topping, plus additional for decorating

10 to 12 mini graham cracker crusts

Mini chocolate chips and chocolate sprinkles

1 Combine sugar, cocoa, flour, and salt in small saucepan. Gradually whisk in milk until blended. Bring to a boil over medium-high heat, whisking constantly. Boil 1 to 2 minutes or until thick custard forms. Remove from heat.

2 Stir in chocolate chips until melted and smooth. Pour custard into bowl; cover with plastic wrap. Plastic wrap should touch surface of custard to prevent skin from forming. Refrigerate 4 hours or until cold.

3 Stir whipped topping into custard just until combined. Spoon custard into crusts (about ¼ cup per crust). Cover tarts with plastic wrap touching custard; refrigerate at least 2 hours or overnight.

4 Just before serving, create ghost on each tart with dollops of whipped topping. Arrange chips and sprinkles on ghosts for eyes and mouths.

Makes 10 tarts

Sugar and Spice
Halloween Cookies

2⅓ cups all-purpose flour

2 teaspoons ground cinnamon

1½ teaspoons baking powder

1½ teaspoons ground ginger

½ teaspoon salt

¼ teaspoon ground nutmeg

¾ cup (1½ sticks) butter, softened

½ cup packed brown sugar

½ cup molasses

1 egg

Colored frostings and sparkling sugars

1 Combine flour, cinnamon, baking powder, ginger, salt, and nutmeg in medium bowl. Beat butter and brown sugar in large bowl of electric mixer at medium speed until light and fluffy. Add molasses and egg; beat until well blended. Gradually beat in flour mixture just until combined.

2 Form dough into 2 balls; press into 2-inch-thick discs. Wrap in plastic wrap; refrigerate at least 1 hour or until firm. (Dough may be prepared up to 2 days before baking.) Let stand at room temperature to soften slightly before rolling out.

3 Preheat oven to 350°F. Roll out dough on lightly floured surface to ¼-inch thickness. Cut out cookies with Halloween cookie cutters. Place cutouts on ungreased cookie sheets.

4 Bake 12 to 14 minutes or until centers of cookies are firm to the touch. Let cookies stand on cookie sheets 1 minute; cool completely on wire racks. Frost and decorate as desired.   *Makes 2 to 3 dozen cookies*

Taffy Apple Snack Cake

1 package (about 18 ounces) yellow cake mix with pudding in the mix, divided
2 eggs
¼ cup vegetable oil
¼ cup water
4 tablespoons packed brown sugar, divided
2 apples, peeled and diced
1 cup chopped nuts (optional)
2 tablespoons butter, melted
¼ teaspoon ground cinnamon
½ cup caramel topping

1 Preheat oven to 350°F. Spray 8-inch square baking pan with nonstick cooking spray. Reserve ¾ cup cake mix in medium bowl.

2 Beat remaining cake mix, eggs, oil, water, and 2 tablespoons brown sugar in large bowl with electric mixer at medium speed 2 minutes. Stir in apples. Spread batter in prepared pan.

3 Combine reserved cake mix, nuts, if desired, butter, cinnamon, and remaining 2 tablespoons brown sugar in medium bowl; mix until well blended. Sprinkle over batter.

4 Bake 40 to 45 minutes or until toothpick inserted into center comes out clean. Cool completely in pan on wire rack. Cut into squares; top each serving with about 2 teaspoons caramel topping. Makes 9 servings

Jack-o'-Lantern

2 recipes Buttercream Frosting (page 246)
  Orange, green, and brown food colorings
2 (10-inch) bundt cakes
  Base Frosting (page 246)
  Candy corn
  Ice cream wafer cone

1 Prepare Buttercream Frosting.

2 Add orange food coloring to 4½ cups buttercream frosting, a few drops at a time, until desired shade of orange is reached. Add green food coloring to ½ cup buttercream frosting, a few drops at a time, until desired shade of green is reached. Add brown food coloring to ½ cup buttercream frosting, a few drops at a time, until desired shade of dark brown is reached.

3 Trim flat sides of cakes. Place one cake on large plate, flat side up. Frost top of cake with thin coat of orange frosting. Place second cake, flat side down, over frosting. Frost entire cake with base frosting to seal in crumbs. Frost entire cake with remaining orange frosting.

4 Frost wafer cone with green frosting. Place upside-down in center of cake for stem. Using medium writing tip and brown frosting, pipe eyes and mouth. Arrange candy corn for teeth as shown in photo. Slice and serve top cake first, then bottom. Makes 36 to 40 servings

Haunted Party Tips

A fall birthday is the perfect opportunity for a party with a Halloween theme. Create scary decorations such as spiderwebs and bats hanging from the ceiling and perhaps a coffin or graveyard scene. Turn down the lights and play a tape of scary sounds to add to the spooky atmosphere. Costumes are required, of course, but you may want to make masks as part of the party. Provide a plain mask for each child and supply plenty of paints, markers, construction paper, crepe paper, fabric, yarn, and glitter.

Buttercream Frosting

6 cups powdered sugar, sifted and divided
¾ cup (1½ sticks) butter, softened
¼ cup shortening
6 to 8 tablespoons milk, divided
1 teaspoon vanilla

1 Beat 3 cups powdered sugar, butter, shortening, 4 tablespoons milk, and vanilla in large bowl with electric mixer at low speed until smooth. Add remaining 3 cups powdered sugar; beat until light and fluffy, adding more milk, 1 tablespoon at a time, as needed for desired consistency.   Makes about 3½ cups

Base Frosting

3 cups powdered sugar, sifted
½ cup shortening
¼ cup milk
½ teaspoon vanilla
Additional milk

1 Combine sugar, shortening, ¼ cup milk, and vanilla in large bowl. Beat with electric mixer at low speed until smooth. Add more milk, 1 teaspoon at a time, until frosting is thin consistency. Use frosting immediately.   Makes about 2 cups

Clever Costumes

Ghoulish Getups

Your favorite trick-or-treaters will be sure to scare up some fun in these spooktacular costumes.

What You'll Need

- Black sweat suit
- Black gloves
- White fabric marker
- White glow-in-the-dark fabric paint
- Small paintbrush
- Nontoxic face paints: white, gray or black

Bag of Bones

1 Using a skeleton illustration as reference, draw bones on the black sweat suit and gloves with fabric marker. Paint the bones with glow-in-the-dark paint. Let dry; paint another coat if necessary for complete coverage.

2 Use nontoxic face paint to paint the child's face white. Paint gray or black around the eyes and mouth.

Haunted Tip

Take apart an inexpensive cardboard skeleton, and use it as a template to trace bones on the sweat suit.

Graveyard Ghost

What You'll Need

- 24×21-inch piece cardboard
- Pencil
- Box cutter or craft knife (adult use only)
- Gray spray paint
- Acrylic paint: light gray, black
- Sponge
- Small paintbrush
- White ribbon
- Scissors
- Hot glue gun, glue sticks
- Black or gray sweat suit
- White twin sheet

1 Lightly sketch a simple tombstone shape on the cardboard; cut out with a box cutter. In a well-ventilated area, spray-paint the tombstone gray; let dry 20 to 30 minutes. Dampen a sponge, and lightly dip it into light gray paint. Sponge over the surface of the tombstone to create a mottled appearance. In the same manner, lightly sponge black paint to accent. Draw "R.I.P." in decorative letters on the tombstone. Paint the letters black; let dry completely.

2 Cut 2 long pieces of white ribbon. Hot glue 1 ribbon to each side of the tombstone at the top corners.

3 Drape white fabric over the child's head to form a hooded cape; trim the bottom if necessary.

4 Tie white ribbons together behind the child's neck to hang the tombstone and to hold cape in place.

Werewolf

What You'll Need

- Black sweat suit
- Black knit hat
- Scissors
- ½ yard brown, black, or blended faux animal fur
- Hot glue gun, glue sticks
- Index card, painted black
- Black or brown shoes
- Nontoxic face paint: brown, black, orange
- Plastic fangs
- Plastic black nails

1 Cut a jagged edge along the bottom of the sleeves and legs of the sweat suit. Cut a 1-inch strip of fur to fit around the collar of the sweat shirt; glue in place. Cut jagged holes in the sweat shirt with scissors, then turn it inside out. Glue patches of fur so the fur peeks out the front of each hole. Turn the sweat shirt right side out. Repeat with the pants. Don't worry about fur shedding on black clothes—the hairier, the better!

2 For the ears, cut 2 pieces of fur (about 4 inches long) into ear shapes; glue them (fur side up) to an index card. Cut out the ears, and glue them to the sides of the hat. Cut and glue a 1-inch strip of fur to fit around the bottom of the hat. Glue pieces of fur to shoes.

3 Use face paints to create a werewolf face. Put on fangs and plastic nails.

Fairy-Tale Fun

Take a page out of your child's favorite storybook for clever costumes that will delight boys and girls alike!

Pretty as a Princess

What You'll Need

- Long-sleeve white shirt
- Assorted faux jewels
- Fabric glue
- 1½ yards pink felt
- Tape measure
- Scissors
- Ribbon: 28 inches pink, 1½ inches wide; 45 inches pink, ⅝ inch wide; 55 inches blue, 1½ inches wide; 70 inches blue, ⅝ inch wide
- Safety pin
- Adhesive-back hook-and-loop tape
- 1½ yards light blue tulle
- Waxed paper
- Poster board
- Pencil

1 Glue jewels onto the white shirt in a necklace pattern. Cut a 27-inch square from pink felt. Glue large jewels along the bottom edge of the felt.

2 Fold ½ inch in the ends of the 1½-inch-wide pink ribbon; glue in place. Glue 1 edge of the ribbon along the top edge of the felt, ¼ inch from the edge. Fold the ribbon over the felt edge, and glue down the other ribbon edge, leaving the center of the ribbon unglued. Let dry.

3 Fasten a safety pin to the end of the ⅝-inch-wide pink ribbon. Thread it through the 1½-inch-wide ribbon already glued to the felt.

4 Cut and glue a 3-inch strip of hook-and-loop tape to the inside and outside edges of the felt to close the back. Pull the ⅝-inch-wide ribbon to gather the skirt around the child's waist; tie the ribbon into a bow.

5 Place the tulle, folded in half as it comes from the bolt, on waxed paper. Glue small jewels to the tulle. Affix the 1½-inch-wide blue ribbon to the tulle as you did with the pink ribbon to

the felt in step 2. Follow step 3 to thread the ⅝-inch-wide blue ribbon. Place the tulle skirt over the felt skirt. Pull the ribbon to gather the tulle around the child's waist, then tie a bow in front.

6 Draw and cut out a crown pattern from poster board. Then trace the crown onto pink felt; cut out. Glue the felt to the poster board, and glue jewels to the crown. Cut a 3-inch piece of hook-and-loop tape, and adhere it to the inside and outside edges of the crown for fasteners.

Bo Peep

What You'll Need

- Frilly dress or floral pajama gown
- 6 yards pink ribbon, 2 inches wide
- Scissors
- 1 yard white lace, 2 inches wide
- Hot glue gun, glue sticks
- Large plastic holiday candy cane
- White bonnet
- Accessories: Lace socks, 3-tiered petticoat

1 To decorate Bo Peep's skirt, cut and glue the pink ribbon to fit around the bottom of the dress and the sleeve ends. Glue lace on the ribbon. Tie a piece of ribbon into a bow, and glue it to the front neck of the dress.

2 Cut 2 yards of ribbon for belt. With more pink ribbon, make a small bow and glue it to the front middle of the ribbon. Make another small bow; set aside. When dressing child, wrap belt around waist and tie in back.

3 Wrap the cane with remaining ribbon, spot-gluing the ribbon to the cane as you work. Glue the ribbon ends in place. Glue remaining bow below the curve of the cane. Add a bonnet, lace socks, and a tiered petticoat for final touches.

Bo Peep's Sheep

What You'll Need

- White zippered, hooded sweat shirt
- White sweat pants
- 10-ounce bag polyester fiberfill
- Hot glue gun, glue sticks
- Square black felt
- Scissors

1 Lay the sweat shirt on a flat protected surface. Use a glue gun to attach small pieces of balled-up fiberfill to the arms, back, hood, and front of the sweat shirt. Cover completely. Repeat for the sweat pants.

2 Cut 2 long ears from black felt, and glue one to each side of the hood.

Creative Classics

Those classic costumes don't have to be dull! Jazz them up for some nonscary Halloween fun.

Clown

What You'll Need

- Hot-pink sweat shirt
- Blue sweat pants
- Sponge pouncer: large, small
- Acrylic paint: green, yellow, violet, white, orchid, hot pink
- Paintbrushes: ½-inch flat, round size 2, shader size 2
- Ruler
- Felt: white, yellow, hot pink
- Scissors
- Rickrack: medium purple and yellow, jumbo blue and green
- Permanent fabric adhesive
- White crochet thread
- Large-eye needle
- 1½×6-inch piece heavy cardboard
- Yarn: yellow, green
- Sewing pins
- White pom-pom trim

1 Wash and dry sweat shirt and sweat pants. Do not use fabric softener.

2 Use large sponge pouncer to sponge green circles randomly on front and back of sweat shirt. Let dry. With end of a large paintbrush, make a yellow dot in center of each green circle. Use small pouncer to sponge violet circles randomly on front and back of sweat shirt. Let dry. Use end of a paintbrush to make white dots on shirt. Let dry.

3 Paint 1½-inch vertical yellow stripes (or make lines depth of band) ½ inch apart across bottom band of sweat shirt. Use end of a paintbrush to make small orchid dots on top of ribbing between each vertical stripe. Let dry.

4 Use ½-inch paintbrush to paint vertical wavy hot-pink stripes approximately 1½ inches apart on pants. Let dry. Paint yellow horizontal dashes across every other hot-pink stripe. Use the end of a paintbrush to make white dots between wavy stripes. Let all paint dry, then heat-set the paint by putting shirt and pants in dryer for about 30 minutes.

5 To make collar ruffle, cut two 42×7-inch pieces of white felt. Fold 42-inch edge over 3 inches on 1 piece of felt and 4 inches on other; pin in place. On opposite 42-inch edge, glue purple rickrack on one piece and blue rickrack on other piece. Let dry. Overlap pieces, and use needle and crochet thread doubled to sew large gathering stitches along folded edges of felt. Pull to gather, and tie around child's neck in a loose bow in back.

6 To make sleeve ruffles, cut two 20×5-inch pieces of white felt. Fold 20-inch edge over 2 inches on one piece of felt and 1 inch on other; pin in place. On opposite 20-inch edge, glue yellow rickrack on one piece and green rickrack on other piece. Let dry. Overlap pieces, and use needle and crochet thread doubled to sew large gathering stitches along folded edges of felt. Pull to gather, and tie around wrist in a loose bow. Repeat for other cuff.

7 To make ankle ruffles, repeat instructions for sleeve cuffs, but cut two 20×7-inch pieces of white felt for each cuff.

8 To make hat brim, cut a 14-inch yellow felt circle, and cut a 6¼-inch opening in center. Cut a 21×9½-inch piece of yellow felt, and glue 9½-inch ends together. Fold top edge of hat over and glue to create hat top. Cut a 21×2½-inch piece of hot-pink felt, and glue around bottom edge of hat as a hatband. Glue blue rickrack in center of hot-pink hatband. Glue hat to brim.

9 Wrap yellow yarn around short side of cardboard 100 times. Slip a 12-inch piece of yarn between cardboard and yarn along short side of cardboard, and tie yarn tightly. Cut yarn along opposite edge of cardboard. Make 2 yellow poms. Trim poms, and pin to front of sweatshirt. Make 3 more poms, using green and yellow yarn. Tie a green-and-yellow pom to each shoe, and glue the third to hatband. Note: If you don't want to go to the trouble of making pom-poms, find large premade poms at your local craft store.

10 Sew or glue pom-pom trim to bottom of sweat shirt.

Gypsy

What You'll Need

- 6 gold foil doilies with solid centers, 12 inches each
- Scissors
- Double-sided tape or glue stick
- Tape measure
- White felt
- Fabric glue
- Adhesive hook-and-loop tape
- Brown paper (such as grocery bag)
- Pencil
- ⅔ yard burgundy felt, 45 inches wide
- Straight pins
- Fabric scissors
- 4 yards gold rickrack
- 2½ yards patterned fabric
- Iron, ironing board
- Liquid fusible webbing
- 1½ yards cording
- Gold cardstock
- Clip-on earring backs
- Accessories: lace scarf for head, black sash for waist, white long-sleeved T-shirt, black tights

1 Cut doilies in half; cut away solid centers. For jabot, you will need 5 doily halves. With first doily half, fold sides back so doily is about 6 inches wide, with gold side on top; adhere sides with double-sided tape or glue stick. For second doily half, fold sides back, with white side on top. Tape or glue as before. Keep repeating instructions until all 5 doily halves have been taped, alternating between gold and white sides.

2 Tape first doily half to back of first, placing it 2 inches below top. Continue until all doily halves have been taped together. Measure around child's neck and add 4 inches. Cut a 2-inch strip of white felt this length. Glue top edge of doily jabot to middle of felt length. Add hook-and-loop tape to ends of strip to close around child's neck.

3 For cuff, layer 3 doily halves, placing each ½ inch below last. Tape doilies together, and trim them so they fit around child's wrist. Make 2. Cut two 2×8-inch strips of white felt. Glue straight edge of doilies to felt. Add hook-and-loop tape at ends of felt.

4 Draw a vest pattern on brown paper; cut it out and be sure it fits child. Pin pattern on burgundy felt, and cut out. Glue shoulders together. Glue sides together. Glue gold rickrack along all edges.

5 Fold over edge of patterned fabric ⅞ inch to form skirt waistband; iron flat. Working

with a small area, apply liquid fusible webbing to edge of folded fabric (be sure you keep channel unglued). Press together, and iron to fuse following manufacturer's instructions. Thread cording through channel of waistband, gathering skirt as you go. Hem skirt with fusible webbing to desired length. Add hook-and-loop tape strips along side edges of skirt. Tie cording at side of waist, and close side with hook-and-loop tape.

6 Cut 2 hoops from gold cardstock, and glue one to front of each earring backing. Make them as fancy as you'd like!

7 Tie a lace scarf (or a remnant of lacy material) around child's head, and tie black lacy sash (or another remnant of lacy material) around child's waist to complete costume.

Haunted Hint
Tie fun ribbons of many colors to a tambourine to complete the gypsy look.

Race Car Driver

1 Wash and dry sweat suit. Do not add fabric softener.

2 Paint a 3-inch yellow vertical stripe down outside of each pant leg. Paint a large rectangle across front of shirt. Paint geometric shapes all over sweat suit and on front of cap using assorted colors of paint; overlap some shapes. Let dry.

3 With fabric markers, write race words in centers of shapes: use words such as Top Pick, Start, Lap, Speed, Drive, Luck, The Favorite, Spoiler, Strong Run, Win, Finish, Tough, Victory, Crew, Go, Fast, and Leader. Paint "Winner" in rectangle across front of shirt, and add vertical stripes before and after word. Paint large purple and thin red horizontal stripes on yellow leg stripes. Let dry.

4 The shorter sides of rectangular box are back and front of car. Cut bottom flaps off box, along with top side flaps and back flap; leave front flap attached. Trim bottom of box to size you'd like car, adding 2 rounded semicircle "wheels" on each side.

5 Turn a longer flap (cut off in step 4) lengthwise, and place long edge along back of box, centering it. Mark box length on flap. Measure and mark lines 3½ inches up from first markings. Then mark horizontal lines out to both edges of flap. Cut along lines, creating a T-shape. Attach bottom of T to inside of car with masking tape. Fold top of T down to make spoiler. (If flap is too long or wide, trim ends or width.) Reinforce folds with masking tape.

6 Bring front flap down over front of box, and mark headlight holes by tracing around plastic containers. Cut out holes. Paint car however you'd like. (Paint front of front flap and front of box same color.)

7 Cut out two 3-inch circles from fun foam. Place plastic containers in front flap holes, and glue white foam circles below them. Cut out a piece of gray plastic to fit around front flap extending about 2 inches on either side. Glue gray plastic to bottom of front flap, and attach extended edges to sides of box.

8 Cut packing foam into 4 strips to fit around "wheels" on sides of car. Spray-paint foam black; let dry. Glue foam to wheels, making sure foam ridges are on outside of wheels. Place car on child, and measure length needed to make ribbon harness. Cut 2 pieces of ribbon this length, and glue ribbon ends to front and back of car on right and left sides to make shoulder harnesses. Reinforce attachment with masking tape.

Animal Adventures

You don't need to go on safari to create your own menagerie at home. These easy costumes will bring out your kids' wild sides!

Elephant

What You'll Need

- Gray sweat pants and sweat shirt
- Size 16 gray sweat shirt
- Scissors
- Ruler
- Adult baseball cap
- Fabric adhesive
- Posterboard
- Pencil
- 2 wood balls, ¾ inch each
- Acrylic paint: black, white, red
- Paintbrushes: ¼-inch flat, fabric bristle
- Hot glue gun, glue sticks
- Peanuts

1 Wash and dry all sweats; do not use fabric softener. Cut a 13×20-inch piece of fleece from bodice of size 16 sweatshirt. Glue to top of cap, gluing fleece edges underneath edges of cap. Add wrinkles for texture.

2 Cut off a sleeve from size 16 sweatshirt. Fold cut edge under, and glue sleeve over brim of cap for trunk.

3 On posterboard, draw 2 large elephant ears and cut out. (Make a 1½-inch long tab on narrow end of each for inserting into cap.) Trace 4 ears on size 16 sweatshirt. Cut out. Glue fleece to front and back of each posterboard ear.

4 Make a 1½-inch slit on each side of cap, 1 inch up from bottom edge. Poke ear tabs in slits, and hot glue tabs on inside of cap.

5 Paint wood balls black, and add a white dot for a highlight on each. Hot glue balls to top of cap for eyes.

6 With bristle brush, lightly paint cheeks, ear centers, and end of trunk red. Glue a peanut to end of trunk, and glue other peanuts to shirt and pants.

Owl

What You'll Need

- Two 2¼-yard lengths of brown felt, 72 inches wide
- Chalk or white fabric pencil
- 1 yard string
- Fabric scissors
- Quick-drying fabric glue
- 1 yard brown ribbon
- Brown knit cap
- Accessories: black or brown tights, white long-sleeve leotard, round glasses

1 Fold felt in half lengthwise. Tie an end of string to chalk. Tie a knot 3½ inches from chalk. To make neckline, hold knot at folded corner, pull string taut, and draw a curve from fabric edge to fabric edge. For bottom of cape, make a knot in string 32 inches from chalk. Again, hold this knot at same folded corner, and draw curve as before. Cut on top line; on bottom line, cut V's along the edge.

2 Fold second piece of felt in half lengthwise. Use 3½-inch knot to make neckline as you did with first. Then make a knot 6 inches from chalk, 12 inches, 18 inches, 24 inches, and 32 inches. Cut on all lines, but cut V's on 32-inch line. At bottom of each piece, cut V's. Beginning 6 inches up from bottom of cape, glue layers onto cape, overlapping each layer slightly. Cut brown ribbon in half; glue to inside edges of neckline for ties.

3 Cut 2 ears from brown felt scraps; make a small vertical slit in bottom of each ear. Fold slit ends over each other, and glue together with fabric glue. Glue ears to knit cap.

4 Wear black or brown tights and a white leotard for the owl body. Add round glasses with black frames for a wise look!

Pig

What You'll Need

- Pink sweat shirt and sweat pants
- Heavyweight paper
- Pencil
- Craft knife
- Black fabric paint
- ½-inch flat paintbrush
- Craft foam: pink, black
- Scissors
- Permanent black marker
- Pink headband
- Hot glue gun, glue sticks
- Black elastic, ⅛ inch wide
- Black chenille stem
- Safety pin
- Duct tape
- Optional: paper towel roll

1 Wash and dry sweat shirt and sweat pants; do not use fabric softener. Write "Oink" on heavy paper in fun, thick lettering. Cut out inside of letters with a craft knife to create a stencil. Place stencil on shirt and pants, and paint letters black. Follow manufacturer's instructions to set paint.

2 Draw 2 ears on pink foam, and cut out. Outline ears with black marker. Hot glue ears to headband.

3 Draw 4 hooves on black foam, and cut out. Poke 2 small holes on either side of each along top straight edge. Tie an end of elastic through each hole, creating a braceletlike attachment. Make sure elastic stretches easily over child's wrists and feet before cutting elastic and tying a knot in second hole.

4 To curl tail, twist chenille stem around a marker. Poke end of stem through back seam of sweat pants, and pin it to inside.

Cover pin with duct tape to protect child.

5 Optional: To make a snout, cut off a 2-inch piece from a paper towel roll. Cut a strip of pink foam to fit around the roll, and glue it in place. Cut a piece of black foam to cover end of roll, and glue it in place. Make 2 small holes in either side of snout. Cut elastic to fit around child's head, and tie elastic ends in holes. Use a black marker to draw nostrils and outline end of snout.

Outer Space Travelers

*For an out-of-this-world idea, dress your kids—
and even the family pet—in space suits!*

Space Alien

What You'll Need

- Gray sweat pants
- White T-shirt
- ¼ yard white fabric
- Craft foam: white, yellow
- Pencil
- Scissors
- Glow-in-the-dark dimensional fabric paint: yellow, orange, green
- Hole punch
- Elastic cord
- 5 styrofoam balls, 2 inches each
- Dark blue acrylic paint
- Paintbrush
- Double-sided iron-on fusible webbing
- Iron, ironing board
- Cardboard box to fit child
- Box cutter (adult use only)
- Heavy-duty aluminum foil
- Tape: 2-inch heavy-duty clear, ½-inch double-sided, duct, yellow electrical
- Hot glue gun, glue sticks
- Neon blow pens: yellow, green, pink, orange
- Flexible vinyl duct, 4 inches wide
- White milk jug
- 14-gauge wire: copper, silver
- 2 wood dowels: 1 inch, ⁵⁄₁₆ inch
- Wire cutters
- Large needle
- Pliers
- 20-gauge wire: green
- Small piece quilt batting

1 Wash and dry sweat pants, T-shirt, and white fabric; do not use fabric softener.

2 Draw a mask onto white craft foam, and cut out. Make sure eye holes are large enough for child to see out. Outline mask using dimensional paint. Let dry 12 hours. Punch holes in either side of mask, and tie ends of elastic cord in holes.

3 Use dimensional paint to draw squiggles on yellow foam. Let dry 12 hours. When dry, cut out around squiggles, creating different geometric shapes.

4 Paint foam balls blue; let dry. Use dimensional paint to make squiggles on balls. Let dry 12 hours.

5 Following manufacturer's directions, fuse webbing to back of white fabric. Draw 4 oval shapes on fabric, and cut out. Fuse fabric to sweat pants, 1 on thigh and 1 on shin of each leg. Use dimensional paint to draw squiggles and dots on fabric. Let dry 12 hours.

6 Use box cutter to remove bottom of box. Cut holes for neck and arms. Cover box with foil using clear tape and hot glue. Use blow pens to add swirls of color to front of box. Use double-sided tape to attach foam shapes to box front. (Save a few smaller shapes for helmet.)

7 Cut 2 pieces of vinyl duct the length of child's arms. Fold plastic to inside, and cover with clear tape. Use clear tape to attach duct to ends of T-shirt sleeves. Stretch duct to full length, and use blow pens to decorate.

8 Cut milk jug below handle, about 3½ inches from base of jug, and continue cutting around jug. Bottom of jug is helmet. Cut slits at corners if jug is too small to fit child's head. Use blow pens to color helmet.

9 Coil 14-gauge wire around 1-inch dowel to make 3 inches of coil with 1 inch of straight wire at each end. Make as many coils as you'd like. Wrap double-sided tape to end of a wire, and stick end into foam ball. Make 3. Poke holes in milk jug with needle. Push ends of wire coils through hole, and use pliers to bend wires flat against jug. Cover wire ends with duct tape. Use double-sided tape to attach foam shapes to helmet.

10 Coil 20-gauge wire around ⁵/₁₆-inch dowel, and attach foam circles to an end using yellow electrical tape. Attach coils to helmet as in step 9. Hot glue batting to inside of helmet to protect child's head. Make moon boots (see Astronaut step 5).

Astronaut

What You'll Need

- Gray sweat shirt and sweat pants
- Dark blue craft foam
- Pen
- Glow-in-the-dark dimensional fabric paint: yellow, green
- Paintbrush
- Scissors
- 8×10-inch piece cardstock
- Heavy-duty aluminum foil
- Tape: 2-inch clear tape, double-sided, duct
- Jewels: assorted colors and sizes
- Metal glue
- Quilt batting
- Baseball cap

1 Wash and dry sweat shirt and sweat pants; do not use fabric softener.

2 Draw 17 stars on blue foam. Use yellow and green paint to outline stars. Let dry 12 hours. Cut out stars.

3 Cover 8×10-inch cardstock with aluminum foil using clear tape. Use double-sided tape to attach stars to corners of foil. Use metal glue to attach jewels. Use double-sided tape to attach foil piece to front of sweat shirt. Attach stars and jewels to arms of sweat shirt and legs of sweat pants in same manner.

4 Wrap quilt batting around cap, filling in space over bill of cap (bill is back of helmet). Cover with foil. Crimp foil under edge of cap, and secure with duct tape. Attach stars to helmet with double-sided tape and jewels to helmet with metal glue.

5 Use foil to create moon boots: Cut a large piece, and wrap around shoe and leg, taping in back to hold in place. Repeat for other leg.

Space Dog

What You'll Need

- 3 foam balls, 1½ inches each
- 5½-inch plastic bowl
- White elastic cord
- 20-gauge wire: green, gold
- 26-gauge wire: hot pink, hot yellow, teal
- Wood dowels: ⁵⁄₁₆ inch, ½ inch
- Flexible vinyl duct, 4 inches wide
- Some supplies from other space costumes will also be needed for this costume

1 Paint foam balls blue. Let dry. Use dimensional paint to make squiggles and dots on balls. Let dry 12 hours.

2 Cover outside of bowl with aluminum foil. Punch holes in rim on opposite sides of bowl. Cut 2 lengths of elastic cord long enough to tie under dog's chin. Tie cord ends into holes in rim.

3 Coil 20-gauge wire around ⁵⁄₁₆-inch dowel, making approximately 3 inches of coil with ½-inch straight ends. Make 3 coils. Cover a straight end of wire with double-sided tape, and push into a foam ball. Repeat for other 2 foam balls and coils. Use large needle to make holes in middle top of helmet. Push other straight end of wires

through holes, and flatten against helmet using pliers. Cover ends on inside with duct tape.

4 Use ½-inch dowel to make 3 coils from 26-gauge wire by tightly wrapping all 3 color wires at the same time around dowel. Spread and twist coils to make approximately 3-inch coils with a ½-inch straight end. Use needle to make holes in helmet and attach coils as you did in step 3.

5 Cut 2 lengths of vinyl duct as long as dog's front legs. Fold excess plastic over cut ends of wire to inside, and cover with clear tape. Stretch duct out, and use blow pens to decorate. Use hole punch to make a hole through top of duct where taped, and tie a length of elastic cord long enough to go from top of one legging over dog's back to top of other legging. Make a hole in second legging. Put leggings on dog, positioning holes at outside of dog's legs. Tie elastic cord through second hole.

Amusing Attire

You'll be sure to make the whole neighborhood laugh with glee when they view these fun costumes.

Cell Phone

What You'll Need

- Large rectangular cardboard box
- Heavy-duty masking tape
- Ruler
- Pencil
- Craft knife
- Red gloss spray paint
- Spray glitter (optional)
- White paper
- Black marker or computer printer
- Scissors
- 12 plastic containers, 4½×6 inches each
- Glue stick
- 2 yards red ribbon, ½ inch wide
- 5×18-inch black craft foam
- Hot glue gun, glue sticks
- Black or red headband

1 Open box flaps, and tape them so they stand up. Measure down 2 inches from top of a flap on a wider side. Cut a 12×7-inch opening for face hole.

2 Below flap fold on same side as face hole, measure 4 rows of 3, making 4×5-inch openings at least 1 inch apart and placing openings lengthwise. Cut out openings.

3 For armholes, measure down 8 inches from top of box sides. Cut out 6-inch circles with a craft knife.

4 Add support with tape to top and bottom of box where necessary. (If the child is short, you may want to leave bottom flaps untaped for easier movement.) Spray-paint box red. Let dry, and spray with glitter, if desired.

5 Draw or print out large numbers using your computer. Make numbers 0 through 9, as well as a star and pound sign. Each number should be approximately 3½ inches tall. Cut out numbers, and use glue stick to attach them to inside bottom of plastic containers. Cut 12 pieces of white paper to size of container openings; glue paper to openings.

6 Push each phone key through back and out front of each opening in cardboard.

7 Cut four 18-inch pieces of ribbon for shoulder straps. Put cell phone on child, and put a mark on the inside of box approximately 8 inches below center of front and back of each shoulder.

Glue an end of a ribbon over each mark. Be sure child's arms fit comfortably through armholes.

8 To make antenna, roll black craft foam into a tube and hot glue it in place. Glue an end of antenna to side of headband.

9 Slide phone over child's head, and tie the ribbons on top of each shoulder. Place headband on child.

Messy Drawer

What You'll Need

- Brown sweat pants and colorful sweat shirt
- Black fabric paint
- Paintbrush
- Long, narrow cardboard box, such as a full sheet cake box, lid detached
- Scissors
- Acrylic paint: brown, black
- Toilet paper roll
- Hot glue gun, glue sticks
- Small, lightweight household items: facial tissue, crumpled papers, notepad, message slips, batteries, puzzle pieces, plastic toys, socks, keys, cards, tape, tickets, stamps, photos, school report cards, letters from teacher, small phone book, crayons, etc.
- Bright baseball cap
- 2 yards wired ribbon, 2 inches wide
- Duct tape

1 Wash sweat pants and sweat shirt. Do not use fabric softener. Paint black lines on pants to create wood grain. (If you can't find brown sweat pants, dye white pants brown. Follow instructions on dye box.)

2 Cut a small semicircle out of back of box for child's body. Paint box brown, inside and out. Repaint if necessary for complete coverage. When dry, paint black lines along sides of box to create wood grain.

3 For drawer handle, cut toilet paper roll in half lengthwise and discard half. Paint other half black. Let dry. Glue it to center front of drawer.

4 Hot glue household items inside drawer. Overlap some items and have others pouring out of sides and front. Randomly glue smaller items to baseball cap. Also glue a few items to shirt.

5 To make drawer easy to tote, cut a slit on each side of box, attach ribbon, and secure ribbon with duct tape. Box will hang like a peanut vendor's box at a ball game.

6 Don't forget to add messy hair to complete the outfit!

Pencil

What You'll Need

- 47×42-inch thin foam
- Ruler
- Pencil
- Spray paint: light brown, yellow
- Heavy-duty aluminum foil
- Scissors
- Permanent fabric adhesive
- Permanent black marker
- Roll adhesive hook-and-loop tape, 1 inch wide
- Roll black elastic, 1 inch wide
- White posterboard
- Acrylic paint: black, light tan
- 1-inch flat paintbrush
- White elastic, ¼ inch wide

1 Measure in 8 inches along 47-inch edge of foam. Spray paint this area light brown for eraser; spray paint remaining area yellow.

2 Cut a 47×6-inch piece of foil. Glue foil above eraser. With ruler and black marker, measure and make horizontal lines 2 inches apart, starting at bottom edge of foil and ending at top edge.

3 With black marker, draw vertical broken lines 4 inches apart across yellow portion of foam. Write "No. 2" vertically on pencil (see photo).

4 Cut a 6-inch length of hook-and-loop tape, and attach it to top of both sides of back of pencil (be sure tape matches up when closing pencil).

5 To make armholes, lay pencil flat with closure in center back. Measure down 5 inches from top, and cut 7-inch semicircles on right and left sides of pencil.

6 Cut two 12-inch strips of black elastic and four 2-inch pieces of hook-and-loop tape. Put pencil on child and make marks on inside of foam approximately 4 inches below center of front and back of each shoulder. Stick hook-and-loop tape inside front and back over pencil marks. Stick other side of hook-and-loop tape along end of elastic so pencil fits child well (trim elastic if needed).

7 To make pencil tip, cut out a large circle from posterboard. Cut out a pie-piece shape from circle, and hold cut edges together to form a cone. Try cone on child's head, and trim if too big. Glue cut edges when it is correct size. Paint cone light tan, and when paint is dry, paint tip black. Cut a piece of white elastic to fit underneath chin, and glue each end to right and left inside of hat.

Phantastical Pumpkins

Monster Welcome

Greet those trick-or-treaters with an eerie glow that can only come from a monster jack-o'-lantern.

Witchy Warts

1 Carve the eyes, then the nose and mouth.

2 Carve the hair next. Starting with the brim, cut out the hat.

3 Use a drill bit to create the wart. If you'd rather not use a power tool, very carefully push a pen or pencil into the pumpkin.

Skully the Skeleton

1 Carve the nose and the eyes, working from the center out.

2 Carve the teeth.

Frankenstein

1 Carve the eyes and the nose.

2 Carve the remaining features, working from the center and cutting outward.

Enlarge patterns to fit pumpkins.

Funny Faces

These happy faces are just right for the younger set or for those adults who like to keep things on the light side!

Traditional Jack

1 Carve the nose.

2 Carve the remaining features. Customize the design by adding or deleting teeth. To simplify, omit the teeth and the irises in the eyes.

Smilin' John

1 Carve the eyes and nose.

2 Carve the mouth and chin. Be careful not to make the connection for the tongue too thin.

3 Carve the eyebrows.

Big Tooth Magee

1 Carve the eyes and nose.

2 When carving the teeth, work from the top down. Be careful not to make the space between the teeth too thin.

3 Carve the brow.

Enlarge patterns to fit pumpkins.

Creepy, Crawly Things

Bats in your hair and spiders in your room...EEK! But no worries. These creatures won't make you squirm—they'll light up your Halloween night!

Batty Flysby

1 Carve eyes, mouth, inner ears, and lines of the body.

2 Starting with the toes of the outstretched foot, carve around the foot, the wings, and the outside of the head.

3 Carve the tree branches and the outside of the circle.

Spindle the Spider

1 Carve the back end of the spider's body.

2 Carve the legs, starting at the center and cutting outward.

3 Carve the fangs and the thread that the spider hangs from.

4 Carve the lettering. To simplify the design, omit this step.

Enlarge patterns to fit pumpkins.

Frightening Fun

Spine-tingling delights are in store for you with these gruesomely ghastly pumpkin carvings!

Howlin' Wolf

1 Carve the nose. If the scrap pieces aren't easy to push out, cut them into smaller pieces to remove.

2 Carve the mouth, being careful not to cut off the teeth.

3 Carve the ears, top of the head, and jowls. To simplify, create the features by cutting zigzag lines and leaving scraps in place. The light from the inside will still shine through the cuts.

Glare Scare

1 Carve the eyes, the eyebrows, and then the nose.

2 Carve the smaller teeth. Finish by cutting the large fangs.

Eye See You!

1 Drill holes for the center of the eyes (or push a pen or pencil into the pumpkin to create the holes). Carve the rest of the eyes and the bottom lashes.

2 Carve the top eyelashes starting at the center and working up and out.

Enlarge patterns to fit pumpkins.

Boo! to You

*Don't let these spooky pumpkins scare you away.
They'll fill your Halloween with ghostly fun!*

Scaredy Cat

1 Start by carving the eyes. To simplify the design, omit this step.

2 Carve the areas between the legs.

3 Carve the silhouette of the cat. Finish by cutting the outer circle.

Ghostly Greetings

1 Begin by carving the eyes and mouth.

2 Carve the letters and the exclamation mark. The dot of the exclamation mark can be created with a drill bit or by carefully pushing a pen or pencil through the pumpkin. To simplify the design, omit the exclamation point.

3 Carve the circle.

Enlarge patterns to fit pumpkins.